Trish Richardson
and
The Soul of Jazz

"Trish Richardson has the unique ability to illuminate the blood, sweat, and, sometimes tears, that goes into the making of a professional musician when the stage lights are off."

—JOSH BROWN, trombone

"This is unquestionably the best-written interview I have ever read of me."

—BENNY GREEN, piano

"Trish's way with words rhythmically dances through her interview with the artist. If you love jazz, I'm sure you will welcome this intimate and introspective jazz journey."

—BILLY KILSON, drums

"Trish is truly a catalyst for thought and is devoted to bringing out the inner workings of those she chooses to write about. I look forward to reading what she has to write in the future."

—MARK SMALL, saxophone

"Trish Richardson is the rare combination of intellect, curiosity, objectivity, and expressive interpretation. Like the blending of ingredients in a recipe, her balance of these key elements is rare, elusive, and deserving of praise and recognition when it is achieved."

—ROB PERKINS, drums

"Thanks for putting your heart and soul into this book. It's something really special you're doing."

—MINDI ABAIR, saxophone and vocals

"Books are extremely inspiring, like music can be. A great book can make people think differently and inspire them and change the way they move forward. Please keep writing books."

—JOHN PATITUCCI, bass

"The article you wrote (for allaboutjazz.com) was quite possibly the best piece that anyone has ever written about me."

—MARK WHITFIELD, guitar

Published in the United States by
Grayson James Press, Seattle.

The soul of jazz: stories and inspiration from those who followed the song in their souls / [interviews by] Trish Richardson—1st ed.
Includes index.

ISBN-13: 978-0615509310
ISBN: 0615509312

Designer: Trish Richardson

Printed in the United States of America.

First printing, 2011.

To order a copy of this book, please visit Amazon.com.

For information about special discounts for bulk purchases, please contact the publisher at info@thesoulofjazzbook.com.

Front cover photo credits: ©istockphoto.com/gustavocano
Instrument illustrations: piano, musical notes (on top of microphone): ©istockphoto.com/dra-schwartz
Trumpet, trombone, guitar, saxophone, bass: ©istockphoto.com/aleksangel
Microphone illustration: ©istockphoto.com/draco7
All rights reserved. Used by permission.

The Soul of Jazz

Stories and Inspiration from Those Who Followed the Song in Their Souls

Trish Richardson

Grayson James Press

Seattle

*This book is dedicated to the dreamers
and to those who believe in them.*

*With special love and appreciation to my mom,
who taught three little girls how to believe in
themselves—and each other.*

THE LINE-UP

THE ACKNOWLEDGEMENTS

Writing is often an individual endeavor. However, this project would not have even been possible without all of you who so generously contributed your time, your support, and your stories. Truly, you have made this book what it is.

Mindi, you have such an amazing spirit and a contagious, positive energy. And you are proof that the girls can hold their own out there with the guys—and do it in stilettos, too!

Thank you, Mark S., for your expertise and support, and for keeping in touch all theses years. Good luck in school.

Benny, you are so open, generous, and willing to let others know how much you care. Those are such wonderful qualities to have. Lee, you were the first (certainly not the last) artist whom I thought I would be intimidated by, but you were so warm and friendly, right from the beginning, that I forgot to be nervous. Thank you for that.

Jane, I love that you appreciate motherhood so much, and you continue to be out there pursuing your dream. Thank you for being a wonderful role model for all of us moms.

To Bucky and Freddy, you are both so young at heart and in

spirit. You have paved amazing paths, and are continuing to do so. You are an inspiration for us all.

Craig, I enjoyed seeing New Orleans through your eyes (and listening to your charming southern accent). Wycliffe, "WTF" has got to be the best editing comment *ever*! Thanks for making me smile. Randy N., you were the first to say yes, and I'm so grateful to you for getting the party started!

Renee, you've already accomplished so many incredible things for someone your age—and I am looking forward to seeing, and hearing, more.

Bob, you are so warm and kind, and such a gentleman. Jason, I had a wonderful time talking with you and enjoyed trading toddler stories. Boney, I appreciate your tenacious spirit and love for your music, a winning combination, for sure.

Randy B., the best way to honor your musical path is by helping to pave the road for those yet to travel down it, which you have. I look forward to hearing more from the next generation of Breckers.

Josh and Mark W., my old buddies, interviewing you was even more fun the second time around. Thanks so much for sharing your stories with me...again.

Rob, you have a wonderful spirit and philosophy of life. Thanks for sharing both. Kendrick, the quote on your drumstick says it all. You are an amazing person.

Peter, I've followed your career from the beginning, and of all the musicians in the book, I've "known" you the longest. So, it means a lot to have you be a part of the project. Thank you for making me realize no dream is too big.

John, I interviewed you at the perfect time. You re-inspired me, re-motivated me, and helped me to remember what was important.

Billy, what can I say? You inspired me to fulfill a dream. I am truly grateful.

You all have made this project so much more than I thought possible.

Extra special thanks to the wonderful family members, managers, and assistants—you all went above and beyond to make these interviews happen, and were such a large part of making this such a wonderful experience. Maxine Harvard, you are so special and you set the bar high. Ruth Pizzarelli, you are a kind, gracious person, and I truly consider it an honor each time we speak. Laurie O'Brien, you are so good at what you do, and your colorful emails brighten my day! Paula Crafton, many blessings to your newest family member. Enjoy it all!

Michael Boosler, Ada Rovatti Brecker, April Brumfield, Bobby Collin, Bill Gaal, Niki Gatos, Bud Harner, Cynthia Herbst, Ngoc Hoang, Louise Holland, Rie Kano, Gary Lee, Heidi Meyer, Terry O'Gara, Rebecca Olstead, Sachi Patitucci, Barbara Rose, and Anna Sala—thank you all for your assistance.

Thank you, Nikki Schilling, for teaming up with me on my promotional tour. You are a rising young talent, and I am honored to be part of your musical journey. Mike Schilling, thanks for supporting Nikki and me in our creative endeavors. And thank you, Carolyn Dale, for giving your time and knowledge—and a great deal of patience—to this project. You added so much to the book, and I hope you know how much I truly value your editing expertise.

iv

Thank you, Linda Conklin and the Columbia Winery, for agreeing to host the book launch party. I could not have asked for a more beautiful location. Your generosity is greatly appreciated.

I am grateful for the use of the artists' websites, as well as the many fan sites out there in cyber-world. I am also thankful for the technological resources of modern times, which helped make this project so much easier: wikipedia.com, dictionary.com, createspace.com, istockphoto.com, amazon.com, allmusic.com, and, of course, allaboutjazz.com. Michael Ricci and John Kelman, special thanks to you both for giving me the opportunity to write for allaboutjazz.com. Your site is one of the best out there.

To my entire family, I love you all so much. Without you, I wouldn't be me. Thank you, Kelly, for helping me find my True Joy. Jim and Grace, you gave me the unconditional love, support, and the time, to make *another* dream come true. (You guys were the first.) I love and appreciate you both so much. We are three—forever.

And thank you to God, for everything.

I thank you all,
With love.

THE INTRO

Jazz. I love that word. I love the way it looks; I love the way it sounds when you say it. And, of course, I love the way it sounds when musicians play it. One of the questions that I asked all of the artists in the book is, "What drew you to jazz?" For me, that would be answered in three words: Harry Connick, Jr. I first saw Connick playing piano on TV, back when we were both about twenty or so, in the late eighties. I was flipping through the channels, while on the phone with a friend. Then all of sudden I saw Connick playing. He was amazing! I told her she had to check it out. And she said, "Oh, that's Harry Connick, Jr. My mom loves him."

I had come from an eighties rock background, and though I enjoyed seeing musicians perform solos (who didn't love Eddie Van Halen's "Eruption"?), I had never seen anybody perform at the level that Connick did. Right then and there, I became a fan. Harry Connick, Jr. made me love jazz before I even knew what jazz was.

The inspiration for this book came, first and foremost, from music. Two concerts in particular were unforgettable. In 2007, my husband and I took our then six-month old to a Michael Bublé concert. Who does that? Needless to say, she cried as soon as the music started, and we wound up spending most of the show in the "quiet room," a soundproof booth located about as far from the stage as possible, while our wonderful seats sat vacant in the nineteenth row. We listened to most of the show through scratchy speakers and joked about how the sound would have been better on a CD in the car. Then, about three-quarters of the way through the show, we decided to give it one more shot and try and bring our daughter back to our seats. What happened next was magical! She actually allowed me to hold her while we danced to the music. My husband was next to me, and everyone around us was having an incredible time. The music was so good—we were in the house of Bublé, surrounded by love, togetherness, and joy.

It also led me to want to find out more, not just about Michael Bublé, but also about the talented musicians who played in his band. That led me to contact Mark Small, one of the saxophone players, and he kindly granted me an interview. It turned into a wonderful conversation, during which I told him, "I want to write a book with you someday." It was one of the those things that, as soon as it comes out of your mouth, you wonder, "Why in the world did I just say that?" But, in this case, several years later, it turned out to be true. Mark became one of the twenty-two incredible artists who agreed to be part of this project. Additionally, he became my go-to person for the book on all things musical when my own knowledge was lacking.

Around that same time, another memorable concert experience came when my sister and I saw Chris Botti live for the first time. I had seen him on TV many times and had followed his career. I was expecting something great, and was looking forward to the show. We saw Botti, who definitely lived up to, and exceeded, our expectations, but we also got to hear Billy Kilson play. (That night, Mark Whitfield was not able to perform for most of the show, due to illness.) Getting to experience Billy's music—and it is definitely an experience—was a defining moment. Billy didn't just play the drums; he became part of the drums. It was like nothing I had ever seen before. Seeing Billy play beside Chris Botti was like going to a fine restaurant, ordering the entrée that you have heard everyone rave about, loving it, and then having the chef bring out the most delicious, unexpected, one-of-a-kind dessert made just for you. That was Billy Kilson.

Seeing Billy out there living his dream, and having so much fun doing it, inspired me to go out and discover what my own dreams were. As soon as I got home, I went online to Billy's website, and found a link for an article about him on allaboutjazz.com, written by Katrina-Kasey Wheeler. I thought, "How cool! *That's* what I want to do—I want to interview jazz artists for allaboutjazz.com." Which, soon after, I did. I had the wonderful opportunity to interview Josh Brown, Mark Whitfield, and Leroy Jones. And as often happens, fulfilling one dream made me start thinking about another—one which you are now holding in your hands.

Botti, Bublé, and their respective band members generated some amazing musical electricity during those shows—and I was definitely plugged in. I wrote the short essay "Soul Music" on my website, www.thesoulofjazzbook.com, with these two concerts in mind. I wanted to try to put into words the feeling that going to these shows inspired in me.

For a few weeks after seeing these concerts, I was filled with such inner peace, happiness, and intense creative energy, it was unbelievable. I would frequently get up in the middle of the night and be inspired to write lyrics for several new songs. It was more than just being happy that I had gone to see the shows—it was *so* much more than that. I had received the energy, spirit, and joy from the music and from the musicians. It was a much better souvenir to bring home than a t-shirt or autographed CD would have been!

Around the same time, I read a book by Charles Grodin called *If I Only Knew Then...: Learning from Our Mistakes*. In it, Grodin had asked many noteworthy people to complete the sentence, "If I only knew then...." It was one simple question, but the answers were so interesting and completely varied that I became fascinated with the concept.

4

I had also started watching the TV series *Inside the Actor's Studio*, hosted by James Lipton, who is one of the best interviewers I have ever seen. He has interviewed actors, directors, screenwriters, and even a couple of musicians for the show. The most interesting part of the show, for me, came near the end, when Lipton would ask the celebrity a set of ten questions. The list was originated by French TV personality Bernard Pivot and based on the Proust Questionnaire. Even with the same set of questions used for everyone, I was never bored. The guests' answers were interesting and entertaining and gave quite a bit of insight into who they were as people. I loved watching the show, and still do.

So, the joy and inspiration from attending a couple of jazz concerts, plus the fun and fulfillment from writing for allaboutjazz.com, plus being entertained and engrossed reading Grodin's book and watching Lipton's show, added up, to me, to writing *The Soul of Jazz.* When trying to describe the book to people, I would say it is like *Chicken Soup for the Soul* meets *Inside the Actor's Studio* for music fans. I wrote a set of questions, my version of the Proust Questionnaire, that I thought would allow the readers some insight into who these musicians are, beyond the boundaries of the stage. How did they get to be where they are? What did they do when someone told them they wouldn't be able to make that dream happen? Did they ever have their own doubts about succeeding?

The telephone interviews with these musicians took place between February 2009 and March 2011. Not every musician (or, more often, his or her manager) that I asked to participate said yes, though a surprising number of them did. I just trusted that the people who felt the spirit and the energy of the book, and resonated with that, would agree.

I didn't know how to refer to myself regarding the book. The term author wasn't quite correct; I did not write this book—the musicians did. I didn't want to use "edited by" or "collaborated with," either. To me, it took away from the creativity and energy that I have tried to instill into this project. So, the copy editor, Carolyn Dale, and I, not so jokingly, came up with the term "conductor." I am *The Soul of Jazz* maestro, conductor to a wonderful, talented group of musicians. I guided them, certainly, but they are the ones who brought life, depth, and meaning to the book.

The musicians' interviews are placed in the book in no particular order. For readers, I didn't want it to feel like an album, where one knows which song is coming up when. Instead, I wanted it to feel like going to a jazz concert (what a concert that would be!), not knowing what to expect next.

The book includes a varied selection of today's jazz musicians, at different points in their professional careers. It includes those who are bandleaders, as well those who are sidemen, although most of the musicians included have been both. These musicians do much more than just provide the audience with a couple of hours of entertainment—they share a part of themselves with every performance. The musicians featured in the book are inspirational and insightful. They are ambitious, determined and courageous. They are educated, intelligent and well-spoken. They are business people, parents, producers, teachers, writers, and entrepreneurs. And, they all love their jobs!

I don't play an instrument, and I didn't want to write about music theory. Many people know far more about it than I do. *The Soul of Jazz* goes beyond the music to focus on the musicians themselves. It is not just about what they play, but also about who they are. Not just about what they've accomplished, but also about how they have accomplished it.

None of them got to be where they are without help from those who had done it before them. I wanted to give them all a platform where they could thank those who have taught them, inspired them, and helped make their dreams possible. The best way to honor the past is to commit to the future, and the greatest way to pay back a gift is to pass it forward. Though I am no longer teaching on a professional level, my commitment to educating and enriching the lives of children is a lifelong one. Therefore, half the proceeds from the book are being donated to VH1 Save the Music Foundation, a nonprofit organization dedicated to reestablishing an instrumental music education program in American schools. For more information about the foundation, visit www.vh1savethemusic.com.

From start to finish, each step of the project has been an incredible learning journey, one that definitely had its share of ups and downs, life interruptions, frustrations, and joys. To you, *The Soul of Jazz* may look and feel like just a book, but to me, it is so much more. It is a dream realized, a life goal accomplished.

So, dear readers, it is my hope that this book, and the people in it, will help you to realize your own dreams and to accomplish your own life goals—to listen to the music in your hearts and to follow the song in your souls.

With peace, love, and joy.

Wycliffe Gordon

Birthdate: May 29, 1967

Birthplace: Waynesboro, Georgia

Main instruments: Trombone, tuba, vocals, trumpet

Other instruments: Piano, didgeridoo

Website: www.wycliffegordon.com

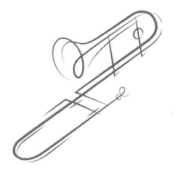

How long have you been a professional musician?

What makes someone a professional is that they're simply getting paid to do a job. My first professional job as a musician was at age fifteen. I played for an Easter service at a guest church in my hometown of Augusta, Georgia. I specifically remember people getting up to leave around noon, and I wondered why there would be a break in the service. Little did I know, the service had ended. Wow! I attended a very Southern Baptist church, and our church would just be getting done with devotional service at this point. These folks were going home already? Nice!

I continued playing music professionally throughout the college years, but my career began with the Wynton Marsalis Septet in June, 1989. It started out as a very good music job that eventually became my livelihood, not something I did every now and again.

Have you had to support yourself with other jobs, or has music been your only profession?

I had other jobs when I was in college. I would go home during the summer and make money doing construction work. Once I started playing with Wynton, performing music was solely how I made my living, and this included composing and arranging music.

What drew you to playing the trombone?

My older brother, Lucius, took band as an elective in junior high school and came home with a trombone one day. With our being just a year apart, I had to have one, too.

We were always exposed to music. My father studied and played classical piano, so piano was actually my first instrument.

I took lessons for two years, but once I got the trombone, it was band all the way!

What drew you to jazz music?

I heard a recording of Louis Armstrong in a five-record set that was owned by my great-aunt. It was bequeathed to our family when she passed away. I listened to this collection relentlessly. It was an anthology of jazz, from the early slave chants to the modern jazz at that time, which included the Dizzy Gillespie Big Band and the Sonny Rollins Quartet. It also had ragtime and New Orleans jazz on it, what some folks call Dixieland. That was my introduction to jazz.

WYCLIFFE'S MUSICAL NOTES

♪ Jazz Journalists Association named Wycliffe "Trombonist of the Year" in 2001, 2002, 2006, 2007, 2008 and 2011, and he is a past recipient of the ASCAP Foundation Vanguard Award, among others.

♪ He is a former member of Jazz at Lincoln Center Orchestra.

♪ He is the youngest member of the Statesmen of Jazz, a touring ensemble featuring senior musicians. In many tour performances, he continues to serve as a musical ambassador for the United States State Department.

♪ *Sing It First,* (Kendor Music, 2011) is a book about Wycliffe's unique approach to technique, and was compiled by Alan Raph.

Who played the most significant role in your musical development? Why?

There were three significant people—my father, my band director, and Wynton Marsalis. My father, Lucius, who was a pianist and local musician, had a profound love for music, and being around this on a regular basis while growing up played a significant role in my desire to be a professional musician.

When I entered the band program at Butler High School, I was very much encouraged and influenced by my band director, Mr. Harkness H. Butler, whom I was with for four years. He was the one who spent the most significant amount of time with me musically during my developmental stages. He nominated me for the McDonald's All-American High School Band during my senior year, and it was being in this band that afforded me future opportunities and experiences both academically and professionally. My sophomore year in college, I met Wynton Marsalis, and what he taught me, and eventually offered me (being on the road with the Wynton Marsalis Septet), was *the most* musically enriching experience I had ever achieved.

There was a time when we were on the road close to three hundred days out of the year, so we were like family. The members of the group became my brothers. The experiences that we had, that we shared—everything from children being born, to birthdays, to marriages, to some of our (and in my case) divorces—we celebrated and held each other together. They were so much an integral part of my growth personally and musically; I think we related to one another's growth from youth into manhood. It was quite a profound experience. As I think about it, I've had many musical experiences since then, but none quite like that with the Wynton Marsalis Septet.

The phrase that we use is "The Seven." We've played with many different people and been in many different situations, but when you are on the road with someone for that long, for that significant amount of time with the same musicians, you begin to know the ins and outs, the idiosyncrasies, of the folks that you are working with.

Is the life that you are living bigger than the one you had envisioned for yourself?

At a certain point in my youth, I remember trying to figure out what was important to me. Was it important to be rich? Was it important to win Grammys? Was it important for me to be the best musician or trombonist according to everyone else's criteria? I grappled with that for, I think, about two or three years. I then settled on: I can only be the best that I can be. I'm not really concerned about someone else's agenda or criteria. I'm doing the best that I can, and that's all that I can do.

As far as awards and recognition, I am thankful for what I have received. I have children, and it is important that I be well received and accepted by all of them. I'm pretty settled with myself, spiritually. I don't expect anything. I feel that if I'm doing well, then I don't need to say I'm doing well. It will be recognized. And even if it's not, I'm not really bothered by it because I know that I'm doing the best that I can.

I live a pretty comfortable life. I'm not even close to being rich, and it is not required. I like being able to do most of the things that I want to do, but I'm willing to work for them. That's how I was raised. We were given very few things, and most of them were the things that we needed. Every now and then, I may get one of the things I wanted. I knew the importance of working to get it, or to make it happen, or to make it available for myself, and not just to expect that it'll come to me.

What have you learned about your character as a result of being in this business?

Character? I talk to my students all the time about being great actors and actresses. But *my* character? I don't know. That's something that I think you would have to ask someone else because it fluctuates, as far as I'm concerned, in different situations and in different places.

I like to think that I'm the same person, no matter where I go. Anytime I'm away from my home or my family, and I am out in the public eye, I have to be a professional. I have to be "on," so to speak. I spend most of my time doing that. But in terms of my character as a person, I don't really get into that until I am alone, or when I am around my family. When no one is looking at me as a musician or public figure, they just see me as Wycliffe, Arnold, or Pinecone.

I spent most of my time growing up while my character as a professional musician developed, and that just simply means I am always conscious of the existence and presence of other people. I try to be nice and courteous to everyone in general. People hold you to a certain standard when you have a little bit of, for lack of a better term, fame. I don't feel like I'm famous at all, but other people do. So I am conscious of what I say and what I do around people. Whereas when I am by myself, or I am in a place where I'm not "on" and being watched, and scrutinized, and that sort of thing, I can just be me. I'll say what I want to say without fear of it being taken the wrong way or misconstrued in any way, shape, or form. That's usually when I'm with my family and my true friends, the people who knew me before I got a job onstage.

Was there anyone who said that you wouldn't be able to make it in the music business—what was your response to him or her?

No. But there were people who didn't have well wishes for me, and they included a few of my professional colleagues. There are several kinds of musicians, just like there are different kinds of people in the world. I choose to be around those who are positive thinking, those who have not allowed themselves to live in a state of being beaten up by the hand that life dealt them. There are professionals who are great musicians, but you meet them, and, as people, they are just so dark and bitter about life. "This didn't happen for me," and, "That didn't happen for me." You know. There are many things that I could think of that didn't happen for me, but I choose to not live on that side of life. I am thankful for whatever it is that I have. I feel like whatever is meant for me, then I'll have it, even if it is not what I thought I originally wanted. So I didn't have many people around who didn't think I could make it. I imagine anyone who didn't wish me well wouldn't be around as much, anyway. I have a great support system with my family and friends.

Our (jazz) community is a pretty small one, and I have encountered musicians that were jealous or envious when I got gigs that they didn't get. "Why did he get the gig? Why didn't I get it?" You know, that kind of thing. There are even people that I've thanked, publicly, for their assistance in turning me on to various things that helped me out as a young musician coming into this profession, who live in this negative type of existence. So, you just have those other kinds of people in the world. I watch them and wish them the best. Thinking like that can be pretty easy to do, but I choose not to.

Were there times when you thought that you might not make it yourself?

I don't remember ever thinking that I wouldn't make it. I remember watching Muhammad Ali as a young boy. He would say, "I'm the greatest! I am the greatest!" I thought, man, he talks a lot of noise. But he talked himself right into becoming what he said he was—the greatest of all time!

What, for you, was the most unexpected aspect about being a professional musician?

Well, there were my young expectations, and there are the expectations that I have now, which are very few. When I say young, I mean when I first got to leave town to go out on the road and travel as a musician. I'd say, "I get to play all over the world. This is great!" I also thought—part of my ignorance in being a youthful male—was that I could be a Casanova of sorts. Wrong! It didn't go down like that—not in the world of jazz. People coming to jazz concerts were mainly couples. There weren't many young people in attendance, although this is beginning to change.

Now, I don't have many expectations, but I understand it is my—our—responsibility as professionals to educate the youth so that they can understand the importance of this music called jazz, and what it did for our culture in the United States. For Americans in general, but also what jazz did for the world culture at large. We Americans were kind of the last to get on board, in terms of recognizing the importance of this music as an art form. I think it was in 1987 when the United States recognized jazz as a national treasure. I had gone to Japan and to Europe, where they were already teaching jazz in the colleges and universities, where they revered and respected the music as true art. You could find jazz recordings in Japan that weren't readily available in the United States. I was like, "What's up with this?"

If you were able, at this point in your life, to leave a note for your younger self when you were just starting out, what would the note say?

I would just say: "Enjoy the ride." If I knew then what I know now, my life would probably be totally different. I mean, I've made mistakes. I've done things that I wish I could go back and change. But that was not the hand that I was dealt. If something were different, then other things in my life might be different now. I am thankful for where I am. I would say to myself what I used to say to myself even when I wasn't aware that I was doing it, and that is: "Enjoy your life to the fullest, young man!"

Music has always been in my life. I've always had that something in my life that I've enjoyed doing. I work all the time, and people ask me, "Why do you work so much?" I tell them that I'm not the type of person who wakes up dreading going to work. I look forward to going; therefore, to me, it's not work. It's not a job. I love what I do and look forward to doing it every day! That's why a lot of musicians are poor business people—because we would all do it for free. I have to make a living. The fact that I get paid to do it, I'm like, "Man, this is beautiful!" When people start complaining to me about things, I say, "Well, you have the power to change your situation. What do you like doing? Figure out a way to do *that.*"

Do you have a favorite quote that inspires or motivates you?

I grew up in the church, and the church was one of my challenges when I started playing jazz. I grew up in the old church-school way of thinking that all secular music was the music of the devil. I'm so glad to see that this has changed, and folks are realizing that all things come from the same source.

One of the Bible verses that helped me to get through is, "All things work for the good of those that believe in God, for those who are called according to His purpose." {Romans 8:28} In other words, to me it means, "It's all good." That's what I believe.

What does music mean to you?

Music is my connection to my highest self. I'm at my best when I'm performing and writing music. It's a way for me to communicate. It's kind of a cliché to say words cannot explain how I feel, but they can't. I don't know the words that can take me to that place.

One of the greatest moments to have experienced was when I was on the road with the Wynton Marsalis Septet. We were with each other every day on the road, so whether or not we were doing one-nighters, the audience would have no idea of how we sounded from day to day, but we would.

For example, Wes [Anderson, saxophone] would be playing, and then he would just go for something. He would start playing stuff that you never heard him play before. It was like, "Man, you were on fire tonight! Everything, all the stars, were aligned."

He said, "Well, I lost the form on the bridge, so forgive me for that sadness."

We were like, "Man, what are you talking about? It was killin'!"

Well, it was, because he went for what he was hearing and didn't quite get it, but what he played was still significant and profound.

Then there would be the moment when it would happen with the whole band. That would be once, maybe twice, a year. Unfortunately, it was never recorded. That's when the band would be playing at such a level that all the stuff would work, and we were all going for it, everybody collectively improvising and integrating. It seemed as though the level of music was so high, you didn't even feel the ground anymore. It was almost like you'd levitate. We would be in the bus after that, and we'd say, "Man, it happened again!" It wouldn't happen often, but the feeling is one I really can't explain. Musically, you are always trying to get back to that. I do have great moments, but the moments like that, even when I talk about them, still bring tears to my eyes.

Lee Ritenour

◆

Birthdate: January 11, 1952

Birthplace: Los Angeles

Main instrument: Guitar

Website: www.leeritenour.com

How long have you been a professional musician?

I grew up in a very lucky situation, first of all. Los Angeles was an amazing music town. It always has been and still is, compared to most cities. Back in the day when I was still a teenager, there were no computers, there were no drum machines, and there were no DJs. So everyone needed a band to play for everything: parties, demos, publishing recordings, real recordings, and live concerts. If you could play your instrument, you could probably work.

My first professional gig was when I was eleven years old. I played at the local music theater and earned six dollars. I was earning money in what we called "casuals" from the time I was twelve.

When I was sixteen or seventeen, I had a chance to do some recordings with various people and even ended up on a recording for John Phillips with The Mamas & The Papas.

LEE'S MUSICAL NOTES

♪ In 2010, Guitar Player Magazine awarded Lee a Lifetime Achievement Award.

♪ He has the nickname "Captain Fingers" because of his manual dexterity on the guitar.

♪ In 2010, he collaborated with Yamaha Corporation, The Berklee College of Music, Concord Records, Monster Cable, and D'Addario Strings to create the annual Yamaha 6 String Theory Guitar Competition.

♪ Lee's musical family includes his son, Wesley, a drummer who was named after Wes Montgomery. Wesley made his debut at age thirteen on Lee's album, *Smoke n' Mirrors* (Peak Records, 2006).

By the time I was just about out of University of Southern California, when I was about twenty, I broke into some more serious work as a studio musician because that was really what I was trained for. I had two dreams. One was to be an artist and do my own recordings, like Wes Montgomery or somebody like that. At the same time, it was a very desirable thing to be a studio musician in Los Angeles and get to work on all these big records and movies. So I wanted to have both lives, and I was actually lucky enough to do both things.

But I was in the union when I was sixteen, so I guess from then on I would be considered to be doing it professionally.

Have you had to support yourself with other jobs, or has music been your only profession?

That's the luckiest thing—there was always a little money coming in from being a musician. And, of course, my parents supported me greatly, and they bought me all these great instruments. They were very helpful, and they got me the best teachers.

In those days, you could look up pretty much anybody in the phone book and get hold of them. I remember my dad calling Barney Kessel, the great jazz guitarist, and telling him what a talented son he had and asking if I could take lessons with him. I did end up taking a couple of lessons from Barney. Then he ended up recommending this teacher named Duke Miller, who became the foundation of all my guitar education. Later, Duke went on to teach at USC when I was a student there. In a way, I kind of introduced him to the school. He was a fantastic teacher.

What drew you to playing the guitar?

It was a long time ago. As a matter of fact, in 2010, it was fifty years that I've been playing the guitar. I still haven't learned how to play the darned thing. But that's what makes it so much fun.

When I first started, I was eight years old and living in Los Angeles. The year being 1960, it was probably one of the most exciting times for the guitar. All of America was into folk music; it was on TV with Elvis and Roy Rogers. A few years later, The Beatles would be coming. The electric guitar and rock and roll were just starting to explode. All the coming sounds that we'd be exploring with the guitar were just beginning. It was kind of the instrument of the day.

But apparently I had a desire to play some stringed instrument because even when I was four or five years old, I was putting rubber bands stretched out on a broom handle with a couple of nails, and then playing the ukulele. So it was always kind of in me to play some kind of guitar.

What drew you to jazz music?

My father was an amateur pianist and had grown up in the Detroit area. He really wanted to be a professional musician, but his parents swayed him away from it during those years. He loved going into the clubs in Detroit and jamming with all the jazz musicians of the time. So there was always a lot of music around my house, and my father really introduced me to jazz, more than anyone.

I remember him taking me to the record store when I was maybe ten or eleven and buying me my first jazz guitar record, which was Wes Montgomery and another jazz guitarist, Howard Roberts, who later I studied with a little bit.

Who played the most significant role in your musical development? Why?

Definitely my dad and my mom influenced me, as well as Duke Miller and Chris Parkening. I also took a few lessons from Joe Pass. Joe and I were actually very close friends throughout the years. Then I was lucky enough to study classical guitar with Christopher Parkening, the great classical guitarist.

So in L.A., and with my destiny, I was very lucky. I had a father who thought about these things and tried to make the best selections for me. I was also lucky enough to grow up in a town where there was work and there were great teachers and other players.

Is the life that you are living bigger than the one you had envisioned for yourself?

Yeah, I guess you could say that. The dreams were not so gigantic. They were in the big, faraway picture: I hope I get to make an album someday on my own, I hope I can make a living, and I hope I can be good enough to be a studio musician. But I was happy just to play in the Disneyland Band for the stage dancers when I got out of high school. I was working six nights a week and making good money. It was cool, and I was happy with that. But after a while, I was not happy with that, either. I had done it and seen what it was like, and then it was time to move on.

I felt the same way about studio work. By the time I was twenty-three, I was earning a lot of money as a studio musician. I could have comfortably stayed in that my whole life, but I had a desire in my belly to make my own music and to control my own destiny. I wanted to try to see if I had my own style and could make my own records and go out on the road. Eventually,

I even cut off a full career as a studio musician. So, after forty albums of my own, I guess it's safe to say that I made it.

What have you learned about your character as a result of being in this business?

I have a very driven personality. I concentrated very hard when I was a kid on making it as a professional musician and trying to be the best guitar player that I could be. I used to practice during the summertimes for eight, ten hours a day. School was a nuisance for me because it just took up so much time when I thought I could be practicing. I was very driven. That drive and that desire for detail, to make everything exactly perfect, have continued throughout my whole life. I spend endless hours on my records, on little details that people say I'm crazy to do. I'm a perfectionist. I'm kind of crazy about the sound on my records. And everyone today, they are listening on their iPods. The newer generation, they don't even care about all that stuff, but I still do. It is important to me. So I do it.

Was there anyone who said that you wouldn't be able to make it in the music business—what was your response to him or her?

The funny thing is, when I was a teenager in high school, my grandmother sat me down and said, "Well, it's nice that you're so talented, but don't you think it's time that you start thinking about something more serious?" My father overheard that conversation and cut her off immediately. He wasn't going to allow her to do that twice.

Were there times when you thought that you might not make it yourself?

I was probably destined to do this, and yet, I had no idea if I could make it. You just never know. I still believe, to this day, the hardest part of being a professional musician is getting in the door. That first "how you become a professional"; "how you wind your way into the business." It seems to be the most nervous time. I still remember that, and I was incredibly qualified. I was much more qualified than I even realized. I was overly prepared, though you can never be overly prepared; but in a way, I was.

I wasn't the son of a professional musician, and I didn't hang out with other professional musicians who had already made it, other than my teachers. And that's different. So you just never know until you get going.

Then after a few years, I thought, "Wow, I'm actually doing this!" With all the challenges that come with fifty years of playing the guitar, I still think, in a way, that is the hardest part. You dream about it as a kid, and you work very, very hard, and you concentrate on it. It becomes your whole life. Plus, it's fun, too. It's what you enjoy doing. We should always keep that in mind. But there comes a point when you are getting out of college, or you are in college and wondering if you are doing the right thing. So it becomes that time of: "Okay, this is it!"

What, for you, was the most unexpected aspect about being a professional musician?

I would say how fluid and ever-changing the business is. Even now, we are in this time when the music business is almost being dismantled and put back together. In a way, it was always doing that. The music business is an ever-evolving creature, like music itself. Maybe it is supposed to be that way.

When you think about the year 1910, there were people who went to the parks and enjoyed music. There was music in people's lives, and people played music at home. There was a piano in the house, if you were lucky. But there was no music "business." There was no structure for selling and buying music. Maybe, occasionally, if someone was a popular artist, people would have to pay a quarter to go see that artist at a little theater. But for the most part, there were no records or anything.

After 1910, or a few years later, there started being structure for recording music, and eventually the music business started. There became a way of selling records.

Today, it is almost 1910 again. The music is in the air, it's free if you want to get it. Every one of my records—and I've written maybe two hundred fifty songs, and maybe over two hundred of them are on my recordings—all of those songs are available for free, if you want to take them out of the air. So, the music business is almost at that stage again where it is being reinvented.

It has been surprising to me, in one sense, that it has deconstructed like this. But technologically, the technical part of the business has kept up with the flow of the music. We went from Edison discovering the sound-through-string, all the way to the CD, and beyond the CD into the computer and downloading music out of the air into digital bits. It will continue to evolve. It went from this beautiful vinyl record to this incredible thing called the CD. It just continually changes, so I've learned to be flexible with it.

My advice to young students is that since you are at the beginning of your careers, you can reinvent the music business. You are at the beginning of a new millennium of music. So, in a way, it is a most exciting time for those people because now there are no rules again. That means you always have to be part entrepreneur and part businessman and part musician. I think that's where a lot of musicians kind of miss the boat a little bit—

they don't realize that it's also a business. When we were kids growing up, we were all lucky enough to fall in love with music and to play music because we have a passion for it. Because we listen to other music, we love it, and we learn from it.

The music business makes it a real business, and that's the part that kills a lot of people. It takes the love and the passion out of it. There's a business aspect of it to keep going. So I think what I've been surprised about for myself is that I've been able to get a balance out of it as far as handling the business and handling the music. It's not easy. Some people have managers; some don't. Some people have a whole lot of people around them to take care of it; some don't. But either way, it has to be taken care of. You have to balance your life so that you can live with that.

Recently, an older guitar friend of mine said he was going to retire, and I asked, "Why do you want to retire?" He replied, "Oh, I want to become an amateur again!" He just wanted to play the guitar and not worry about anything.

If you were able, at this point in your life, to leave a note for your younger self when you were just starting out, what would the note say?

I would probably advise myself to keep things simple. Keep life more clear. Don't worry about every little detail. This is probably advice for all of us—we worry about things that seem so huge at the moment but that later don't seem very big at all.

Also, I might have bypassed the studio-musician step. I kind of bounce back and forth on that thought, wondering if it would have been better. There are a couple of other people in my age group who were studio musicians who went on to have careers, and there were a couple of other musicians in my age group who just concentrated on being an artist. I sometimes wonder what would have happened if I had done it another way. But it was my way.

I think some of my longevity had to do with being a studio musician because I learned so much about so many different styles of music. I keep blending and borrowing and putting different herbs and spices in my music from different walks of life and styles and genres. I got that from being a studio musician, so I don't have too many regrets about the path I took.

Do you have a favorite quote that inspires or motivates you?

There's a quote that I copied on my phone because I like it so much: "Record companies are like flies; they eat honey or s**t with the same enthusiasm." One thing that has changed radically is that when I was first entering professionally into the music, and I was dealing with all the different aspects of everyone who is not actually a musician, but who has something to do with your being a professional musician, in those days, in the 1970s, almost all those people were ex-musicians, from the president of the record company on down the line. The presidents of record companies were all one-time songwriters or drummers or guitar players. Perhaps they were not good enough to be professional artists, but they were passionate about music and good at business, so they wound up running the record companies. They ended up being the producers, the arrangers, the production people, and the contractors, even the lawyers.

I remember one lawyer who came up to me at an event a few years ago. Everyone knew who he was because he was the most powerful music attorney in Los Angeles—a very scary guy. He was very powerful, and he'd worked with every major superstar imaginable and had the power to make or break them.

This guy stopped me as I walked by and said, "Lee, I don't think you remember, but we went to school together at USC.

You are the reason I stopped playing guitar. I wanted to be a professional guitar player, and when I heard you play, I realized I wasn't going to be good enough! You gave me lessons at school, and you told me that if I didn't have the ability to do this part on the guitar, I was really going to have to take a step back and get that part together. That's when I reflected that I really didn't have it."

So, apparently I was kind of hard on him at the time. But he went on to, obviously, do what he did best.

What does music mean to you?

It's my blood. It's everything to me. Without music, I'm not sure I'm the same person on the planet. I have a fifteen-year-old son who has enough talent that he'll be a professional musician if he wants to, which is completely up to him. I see all the same things driving him that drove me. That love and passion are still there for me.

Rob Perkins

✦

Birthdate: January 17, 1975

Birthplace: Dayton, Ohio

Main instrument: Drums

Other instrument: Piano

Website: www. robertperkinsmusic.com

How long have you been a professional musician?

Since I graduated high school, when I was either seventeen or eighteen. I came from upstate New York, then I came out to Los Angeles, and I wound up supporting myself with music.

Have you had to support yourself with other jobs, or has music been your only profession?

During my first year of university, I worked at the university bookstore for the first half year. Other than music, that's the last "job" job that I have had. It's been a good run so far, one very much born out of necessity, but a lot of good fortune as well.

What drew you to playing the drums?

The way I got started was pretty random. I knew my mother's brother was a drummer. My father had played some drums when he was in the military. I'd always sort of thought about the drums and liked them. My family moved from Ohio to New York when I was ten years old. My best friend from Ohio sent me a letter shortly after we moved, and he told me that he had just started taking drum lessons. So that was that. I said, "Okay, I want to go and take drum lessons."

I recently found out that he only did it for about two weeks, that he took two drum lessons, and that was that. And here I am, all these years later. Had it not been for him saying that he had started taking drum lessons and thought it was really cool, I probably never would have thought to do it. Life hinges on stranger things.

I never set out to make a living as a professional musician. I'd always had it in my head to go to law school or maybe go to West Point. I came from a bit of a military family. I have brothers in the military and my father served in both the Marines and the Air Force. When I moved away from home and came to the University of Southern California, I learned that through gigging I was able to make cash in hand quickly—and I needed cash in hand! I didn't have the luxury of waiting two weeks for a paycheck, so I had to find work that paid cash in hand. The fact was that I needed the money, and music paid that night. One thing kept turning into another, and it went further and further. That distinction in the timing of the pay proved to be decisive both in the short and long terms.

When I started university, I intended to major in political science and music because I had a music scholarship. My intention was to double major and then eventually apply to law school. As I got busier and busier, I started taking fewer and fewer poly sci classes. There was also a bit of disappointment from some members of the music faculty when they learned that I was using their scholarship money to work towards a poly sci degree. I was aware that the people in charge of my scholarship were less than thrilled. Then at graduation, I was sitting

ROB'S MUSICAL NOTES

♪ Rob has studied with master drummer Michael Carvin and has earned both a Master and Bachelor of Music degrees from the University of Southern California.

♪ He has been fortunate to travel the globe playing the drums for world class-artists.

♪ Rob lives in Los Angeles with his wife, Shelley, and dog, Aretha, where he continues to play the drums, invest in real estate and other business opportunities, and drive to the airport for worldwide tours.

thinking about what was going on and thought to myself, "I didn't really mean to graduate with a music degree!"

I had work lined up, things to do, and rent to pay, so I just sort of charged off into it. I definitely went through a crisis later of, "What did I do?" But I just kept plugging forward. With the ambitions that I have, and the competitive energy that I have, I was pretty sure that whatever I did, I was going to do okay.

What drew you to jazz music?

I'm not sure, honestly. If I really thought about it, it's probably because my dad used to listen to jazz all the time. It would be on in the car as we were driving around. It was either that or National Public Radio. I definitely didn't like jazz at first, but I came to like it. I didn't distinguish it as being one style that was different from other styles, it was just music that I didn't necessarily like so much at the time. But I definitely came around!

It was a much more active listening experience, listening to jazz. I think it is something that people have to learn how to listen to, especially for people who haven't listened to anything other than concert music. People who were brought up listening to classical or even composed popular music, rather than improvisational, may hear jazz for the first time and not understand it. Anyone, whether they are younger or older when they first listen to it, may not quite know how to appreciate it. But it is something that can be learned.

Professionally, just after I graduated high school and moved to Los Angeles and was supporting myself, I figured out very quickly that with jazz there's room for a middle class type of income. You can make some money that night and walk away and have some cash in your pocket. I feel that with other more popular styles of music, you are making lots and lots of money, or no money at all. When I realized some faster money could be made playing jazz if you did it well enough, I found myself doing more and more of it, out of necessity and because it was something I enjoyed.

I think something happened in jazz, at some point, when looking forward became taboo. This was definitely a nineties thing when jazz became very backward-looking. Really, though, jazz was made by rule-breakers. It's the biggest traditional rule-breaker there is. All of the giants of jazz have been known for breaking rules. Now we call them boundaries, but really they were the rules of the time. Admittedly, it went way too far with the excess that happened with some fusion. I can understand everyone saying, "Okay, we've taken this too far. It's just getting weird; we should go back to some traditions," because things got a bit carried away. But the rule-breaker stopped being encouraged for a little while, which I think is a mistake.

I think jazz is in a really good position, now. It's gone back to a really good position because there are a lot of good rule-breakers around. These are the people who didn't fall for the trap of the super-traditional stuff through the nineties. A lot of the guys who are modern-sounding superheroes now are the guys who didn't fall for that stuff then.

Who played the most significant role in your musical development? Why?

I feel that there's two ways to answer this question: the easy answer and the more challenging answer. The easy answer, say from a drummer, is responding with your usual list of the drummers that you studied. You respond, as every drummer should respond, with a list of your important food groups: your Max Roach, your Art Blakey, your Roy Haynes, Tony Williams, Elvin Jones, and Ed Blackwell. They are most of your essential food groups. You *have* to respond with those guys.

But I think the more challenging response is not the stuff

that you just listened to, but the stuff that you lived around. That really seeps into you early. That's how it worked for me; your friends and your peers, and the guy you used to go see at a club every week in row, the stuff that you really lived around translates into what you do.

A drummer that I used to go and see play at every opportunity was a guy named Eric Harland. I first really got to know him when he played in Terence Blanchard's band. There were, obviously, the major food groups that I listened to, whose stuff I transcribed. But then there was going to see certain guys play sometimes three or four nights a week just because I loved what they did, and they were there and accessible. When I first moved to New York, I was around people like Eric Harland, Willie Jones III, Jeff Ballard, Joe Farnsworth, Leon Parker, Bill Stewart, and Joe Strasser, just to name a few. There were others, but I'm aware that I'm more a product of people I know and have heard personally than of the records that I have studied. And trust me, I've studied a whole pile of records!

When I first moved out to Los Angeles, Billy Higgins was still here, and he had a place down at The World Stage. I used to go there and spend as much time around Billy as I possibly could. He is both a musical and a life influence on who I am. Billy is definitely one of the biggest influences.

Then Michael Carvin, I would have to say absolutely, one hundred percent. And also this drummer named Ndugu Chancler. I am trying to keep my influences to people that I know personally and interact with and was influenced by in a very meaningful way. These are people that I've studied with, who are teachers of mine. So I learned from them that way and also just from being around them and getting to know them. These are both musical and life influences.

Is the life that you are living bigger than the one you had envisioned for yourself?

To be honest, I was picturing, and am still picturing, something bigger. When I was younger, I was picturing something completely different from this. I was planning on being either a senator or some sort of corporate attorney. Then at some point, I got caught up in just wanting to be a bebop drummer and carve out a nice middle class life for myself. Then I came back of that and said, "Okay, I want to be an investor, and a business owner, and sort of a super-capitalist at some point."

I've always had large ambitions, which started with my dad and then came from myself. I was planning on West Point, serving some time in the military, going to law school, running for local office, and then for Congress or the Senate. I was pretty young, but that's just how we saw things. We grew up in a pretty economically challenged household. My father, being a very military type of guy himself, just taught me to be the absolute best student, the absolute best athlete, because that will get you into West Point, which will get you a life in this world. To us, the military academies are where the leaders of American life come from, whether they are political leaders or business leaders. It's what my father taught me. I'm very glad I didn't end up in the military, though I respect and honor those that do.

What have you learned about your character as a result of being in this business?

From the business side of being a professional musician, what I've learned about myself is that I am very sneaky, sneakily courageous, while being pretty shy at the same time. I can be painfully shy, at times, about engaging with people, or calling people, and doing the networking and the things that need to be done. I can be incredibly shy about doing that. I wish I weren't, but because I know I am, I force myself to do it. If I'm not careful, I've noticed that I will find a way to not do it.

I've learned that I have great ambitions, professionally, and I'm really good at putting together strategies to achieve those ambitions. But still I can be painfully shy about some of the things that are necessary professionally to do. It's definitely something I want to be better at. But, at the same time, I have to make sure I do it in ways that I'm comfortable with.

Was there anyone who said that you wouldn't be able to make it in the music business—what was your response to him or her?

Yes, both directly and indirectly. You know how some people can voice their opinions without necessarily putting words to it? Strangely enough, of all people, one of them was my uncle, who was a drummer. I was really into athletics as a student, and I was really big into football and track and field. My uncle had worked a lot as a drummer. It wasn't the only thing he did, but he spent a lot of time playing the drums. He's actually the person who gave me my first set of drums. At one point, maybe my sophomore year of high school, he said, "You know, forget about this music thing. You should be a professional athlete." Of all the things! That was his advice to me. Usually it's: "Forget about this music thing, you should go and be a doctor, or something like that!" I think I was old enough by that age to know that if I'm going to take one risk, I'm going to take a slightly more calculated risk with music. For a professional athlete, it is either do this absolutely, or not at all. So that's one conversation I'll always remember of someone maybe advising me against it.

I remember my father having a conversation with me. He didn't necessarily say, "I don't want you to do this." Instead, he sat down with me and said, "Well, how much do you think you would make, and how much do you think you would need? What kind of work do you think you'd be doing? What kind of life do you think you'd be having?" I was maybe sixteen or seventeen years old, and I didn't know any of the answers. So I tried to put on a good face and answer the questions with as much intelligence as I could, but I very much kind of BS'ed my way through the conversation! I didn't know anything. At the time, I was in high school and was waiting tables at a nearby restaurant. So, for a couple of years, I'd actually been making money at doing something, for the first time. I just thought that money is easy to make, so nothing will ever be a problem. You don't have any sense of relativity at that age. You can go to a movie and buy a CD—what else is there?

I thought, when my uncle said that, there was no way I was going to be a professional athlete. I just didn't see that as a possibility. With other people, with conversations where I saw some resistance, I'm definitely the personality type that redoubles my efforts in facing that resistance. So, whenever I was sort of discouraged, that would only strike a certain stubborn bone in me to keep going. I'm an extremely competitive person, which was part of being an athlete. So I only knew how to respond to that energy in one way. It wasn't through anything else; that's how you're taught to respond to things.

As a younger person, I thought the thing that would fuel me more long-term would be the competitive aspect. But now I have a bit more security financially, and I'm a little more secure emotionally and mentally. So I am not as easily, maybe, pushed either one way or the other. I respond less to input in general now. Whereas then, if there were a criticism, it would be all I would dwell on and just think about, and think about. Dwell on it and compete against it. As a younger person, when you are just trying to prove yourself, and, whether you are admitting it or not, seeking approval of others, you can react very strongly to what people say. I can think of examples when I was probably reactive far above and beyond what was necessary, pushing my way through something I didn't even really have to do.

For a period of time, I was focused on being a traditional, very traditional, jazz drummer. I think I spent so much time doing that because I was told at some point I couldn't. It ended up being very good for me, but I realized that I didn't want only to be that. As with many things in the world that you are doing with a puritanical sort of mind-set, one often thinks that is all that one can do, or it has to be a one hundred percent kind of thing. I definitely spent some years working that way, probably longer than I had to. But I definitely got a lot out of it, and I got a lot of good things from it. But that was definitely one time when I was excluded from, or told that I wasn't going to be able to do, such and such, and I really charged in a certain direction to prove that I could.

I am still a very competitive person, but I'm not as swayed by external stimuli. I'm no longer seeking the acceptance, or the slap on the back, or whatever it is. There are definite decisions that I realized I had to make for myself and not for other people. The decision to join Michael Bublé's band was a really, really tough decision. At the time, I felt that, by joining, I would probably enrich my life in many ways, but I would definitely not get the approval of many of the more purist type of people that I knew or was associated with. I thought I would lose their approval and lose out on working with them, or not work with them as much. So there was definitely a decision there, when I had to go and do what was best for me. It was a good decision. Musicians are strange. Some people were like, "Oh, you're out playing that kind of music now." They consider it more pop. They consider it more commercial. They consider it more schmaltzy or more cheesy, or whatever they consider it to be—they have an image of it.

I had an image of it before I joined, before I got in there and saw what was going on. I even had an image of it that was probably more in line with how they felt, until I got to know it. At the same time, people later on would call and say, "Hey, if a certain chair in that band ever opens up, call me." And sometimes it would be the same people. They would start off thinking one way and go on for a couple of years, and then life gets challenging, and they start planting seeds of, "Let me know if something ever opens up over there."

I'm really, really thankful that during the time that I was trying to make that decision, I was studying with Michael Carvin. I went to him and asked what I should do, really, really hoping that he would tell me! He told me, "You have to make that decision for yourself. You can't ask me to make that decision for you." I really wanted him to, but he stayed out of it one hundred percent.

I didn't make the decision until I actually walked in the room to audition for the band. I stood outside of the building for about ten minutes, just kind of staring at it, and deciding whether I was going to go in or not. I was just trying to make that decision. I really wanted to walk away. I really, really wanted to walk away, but I'm glad I made the decision to walk in and do the audition.

Were there times when you thought that you might not make it yourself?

I always thought I had it in me. Sometimes I doubted whether that's what I wanted to do. I really, really felt that it was something I could do. This is a very unpopular sentiment for musicians to express. Usually you hear: I knew I wanted to do this since I was nine years old; it's all I ever wanted to do, and I can't imagine doing anything else. I feel like that's their story. I have my theories about that story, but that's their story. For me, there often were times when I would question whether it's what I wanted to do. But I definitely felt like it was something I could do. Especially when you are younger in life, I subscribe to the philosophy that if it's something that you want to do, go out and do it. You can find a way to do it.

You can't say that if you play it safe, go to school, go out and get a job, and study hard, that everything will be okay.

That's just something that I really disagree with, and we've seen recently that's not true. There are people who played it safe, got jobs on Wall Street, or graduated with MBAs, who lost their jobs. They played it safe, played by the rules, and they were just put into a terrible position.

I see being a musician as being a business owner. You are then in a position where how profitable your business is, really is up to you. You have some control over it. There's a place for you to place your ambition. When you are just an employee in someone's company, you're totally at their whim. There's nowhere for you to really place your ambition, and if things take a turn, and they need to cut you away, they'll cut you away. That's just how it is. So take away the sense of security, and then you have to ask yourself whether or not you actually like the job, you know? I very much enjoy what I do. I've learned to balance it with other things in my life, and I very much enjoy what I do. Being who I am, I am learning to balance music with my other interests. At the time when it was the only thing I did, and all I did, and I had to absolutely be the best at all times, I wasn't happy. Now I've learned to balance it with other things, and I am really able to enjoy it for what it is.

Financially, I don't think you need to struggle to be a musician. I think you need to work extremely hard. But I think you need to work extremely hard at everything that you do, and you need to work smart. You need to be relentless. You need to understand that if you are in music, and that's how you earn your living, you are going to have to do things to earn a living that are salable. You can't just make music that nobody wants to hear and then sit around and complain that you're not making a living. It's going to be a struggle, but if you are working smartly, it will be a fruitful struggle. If you are struggling financially, it's because you are not working wisely. And that's a difficult position to defend. For example, someone says, "I'm the absolute best tenor player in Fargo, and I'm doing everything right. I'm playing music that people want to hear, and I'm doing it, and I'm making all the right decisions." But you are in Fargo. You have to take your business where there is a market for your business. There are a lot of decisions that fall into working wisely. So, I don't believe that musicians by definition have to struggle financially. You just have to work wisely and expect to have something that is salable if you want someone to buy it from you.

I've had so many people say, "You're so lucky to do what you love." I've heard people say that to other musicians and artists, as well. I just think it's ridiculous—I realize it's easy for me to say—just go out and do what you love. But I think it's a matter of loving what you're doing, whatever it is that you do. Am I lucky to be doing what I love to do? I think that even if I were doing something else, I love the act of doing a job well, whatever the job is. I love the act of working hard at something, of working at something with integrity, and working at something with all the right intentions. The actual task at hand, I think, is irrelevant. I think it is the spirit with which you approach it. There are people who can be musicians or dentists or whatever, and if they are determined not to be happy, they are going to find a way not to be happy. We all know some incredibly wealthy people who are incredibly unhappy. I don't buy into the philosophy of, if you had a job like mine, then you would be happy. The actual task that you are doing is irrelevant.

Even still, there are times when I just not playing as well as I'd like. One of the things you hear professional athletes say all the time is that they are just trying to let the game come to them. Very often, the thing for athletes and their operational state-of-mind, and for musicians and their operational state-of-mind, the thing that can mess that up, is trying too hard, just trying to force it. Just trying to make it happen, make it happen, make it happen. Then that just doesn't end up leaving any room for opportunity to step in, or for creativity to step in. So very often, the biggest thing is to relax, settle down, and stop trying to force it.

Obviously, a state of grace is difficult to achieve. It's grace that people love to hear, see, or witness. And that's what people love about performance—that in some way, there's this great balance between grace and ability. There is this balance between the grace that shows you that they're not trying so hard, and there's that ability that shows you that they are capable.

What, for you, was the most unexpected aspect about being a professional musician?

Traveling the world has changed my sense of America's place in the world. It has been particularly interesting in the fifteen years or so since I've really been traveling internationally. Watching the way the world relates to us through the Bill Clinton, George Bush, and Barack Obama presidencies has been very interesting.

If you were able, at this point in your life, to leave a note for your younger self when you were just starting out, what would the note say?

To move in a straight line, in life and career-wise. To try to move in a straight line and not zigzag so much. I've done a little bit of zigzagging between New York and Los Angeles, and jazz and not-jazz. It's worked and been fine, and maybe I wouldn't be where I am, had I not done it that way.

Do you have a favorite quote that inspires or motivates you?

I once saw a guy in New York City wearing a t-shirt that said "NYPD Bomb Squad" on the front. On the back it read: "If you see me running, you should catch up." I've always made it a point to keep my eye out for that guy. If I see him running, I'll probably try and catch up.

What does music mean to you?

Music is circular. And when it's not circular, it doesn't feel very good. And music is just fun. The older I get ,and the more responsibilities I have, the more the music part is just fun. What really helps the musical part of my life is knowing I will sit down to play just to have fun because I've been looking forward to it all day.

Jane Monheit

✦

Birthdate: November 3, 1977

Birthplace: West Islip, New York

Main instrument: Vocals

Other instruments: Piano, clarinet

Website: www.janemonheitonline.com

How long have you been a professional musician?

I had my first gig at a wedding when I was sixteen. I think I made around two hundred dollars, and I thought it was more money than anybody in the world had ever seen.

Have you had to support yourself with other jobs, or has music been your only profession?

I've never had any other job. I've only ever sung for money. I've never done anything else. Never even babysat—nothing.

What drew you to singing jazz music?

JANE'S MUSICAL NOTES

♪ Jane has been a professional singer since age sixteen. She has never had another job, even though she interviewed for many.

♪ Her first album *Never Never Land* (Encoded Music, 2000) stayed on the Billboard Jazz Chart for more than a year, and it was voted by the Jazz Journalists Association as the top debut recording.

♪ Jane's duet single "I Won't Dance" (*Taking a Chance on Love*, Sony, 2004) with Michael Bublé peaked at number eleven at the World Jazz Top 20 Singles Year-End Chart (2004).

♪ Her trademark song is "Over the Rainbow" from the movie *The Wizard of Oz*.

I just heard the music my entire life, from the time I was a baby. It was part of my existence growing up, and it was the most natural thing in the world for me to study music and to make a living performing it.

My dad is a bluegrass musician, and my mom is a choral singer. I'm pretty much one of the only people in the family who is a professional musician, though. My brother is, as well; he is a rock guitar player.

There were no defining moments for me. Everything was just this super, natural progression for me. I never had any really big epiphany; it just sort of flowed for me from the time I was a little tiny kid. It's just always been this—the jazz singer. It's a really cool thing. I've never had moments of wondering who I was going to be, or what I was going to do. But at the same time, there were never any big "aha" moments, either. It's just always been this. I've always been this person. It's just been this very simple thing, my entire life.

Who played the most significant role in your musical development? Why?

First and foremost, Ella Fitzgerald. Ella was the biggest influence and will always be the biggest influence. I listened to her records nonstop for my entire childhood. I still love her now. But there have been a lot of other singers, as well: Sarah Vaughan, Carmen McRae, Mel Tormé, Keely Smith, Helen Merrill, Take 6, New York Voices. And then people outside of jazz: Barbara Cook, Bonnie Raitt, Joni Mitchell, Stevie Wonder, Judy Garland—a lot of great singers.

In 2009, I was singing in Feinstein's in New York, and one of the tunes that I had been singing a lot was "By Myself." So I do the tune, and I'm sitting out signing CDs after the show, and who walks up, but Helen Merrill. That was a major tune for her.

I said to her, "Oh my gosh, you're here, and I just sang 'By Myself.'"

She replied, "I can tell you've listened to my recordings."

I said, "I certainly have!" There are still moments like that, when I feel like a little kid.

Is the life that you are living bigger than the one you had envisioned for yourself?

I think it's probably about the same. I don't really recall having any specific dream. I've always lived in the moment with those things. I was never one of those kids who said that I want to grow up and get married and have kids, or I want to do this or do that. I was always just focused on what I was doing at the time. So I don't really remember having a specific wish for my future career. I just knew I was going to sing. I knew it was going to happen somehow, and whatever way it happened, it was going to be cool. So I feel very lucky to be making records and touring. I'd be just as happy if I were doing local stuff. And who knows? It may be that, one day. That would be fine. I'm just happy to be a musician because I realize it is such a rare thing. I grew up with hundreds of talented musicians who are doing other things today. I'm one of the only ones, one of the very, very, very few. I could maybe think of one other person I grew up with who is actually a musician now. So I realize I should be thanking my lucky stars, here!

What have you learned about your character as a result of being in this business?

I've learned that I have confidence in myself that is basically unshakable—which is a great thing to know—at least in myself as a musician and in my abilities as a musician. It doesn't always apply to other areas of my life, at all. I know that if I'm singing, I never have to be afraid. I can walk on stage at the most important hall in the world in front of any human being you could possibly imagine, alive or dead, and sing, and not be afraid. It's pretty amazing.

But you ask me to do anything else, and then I lose confidence a little bit, like anyone else would. I've always been close to that level of confidence, but now I am really *here*. It has grown with experience. It's just something that comes to you over time.

Honestly, having a baby has made me even more of a confident person. It makes you let go of stupid little things. I care so much less about being perfectly beautiful, silly things like that. Being a mother is the most important thing you could ever do in this world. It's so much more than anything else. So if I am doing a good job at that, and I am still getting on stage and singing, then everything's cool.

Was there anyone who said that you wouldn't be able to make it in the music business—what was your response to him or her?

I never met a single person, thank goodness. I was surrounded by wonderful, really supportive, amazing people from the time I was a baby. If anybody thought that, they never have said it to me. Even my teachers in school, everyone I was around—it was amazing. It gave me a lot of confidence when I was a kid, which I still have today. I realize exactly how lucky I was.

Were there times when you thought that you might not make it yourself?

Oh, every day I have thoughts like that. Thankfully, they are fleeting, and the rest of the time I say, "Oh, I can do this.

I've been doing it since I was sixteen, I'll just keep doing it, and everything will be cool."

What, for you, was the most unexpected aspect about being a professional musician?

That's easy—everyone making such a fuss over my looks. I can't stand that! I was constantly being told that I'm not pretty enough, or I'm not thin enough, and all that sort of nonsense. I thought that becoming a jazz musician, that sort of thing wouldn't be part of the picture, that it would be about my musicianship—that I was a singer and a performer. I didn't realize that the first time it happened would be someone telling me I was fat. That was a hideous surprise! And now, if anyone talks to me that way, I just don't work with them anymore.

They Photoshop me thinner in every photo, and I'm done up by hairstylists and make-up artists. None of those pictures are really very accurate. I've even had someone change the color of my eyes with Photoshop! When you see me up on stage, that's who I really am. And I feel great about myself! So I have no problem with how I look, and I never really have, until everyone started telling me that I should be having a problem! Then I had a few years of just misery because I felt so ugly all the time. There was lots of being upset all the time, and tears, and everything else, and running off into the ladies' room crying because someone said I looked fat, or whatever. But now, now that I've had a child, you wouldn't be able to print what I would say to someone who would talk to me that way.

I never even used to be able to talk about it. The whole thing was so horrifying for me that if anybody even dared bring it up in an interview, I would be so uncomfortable, I would just turn into a wreck. And now I would like the world to know that anyone who has a problem with me is completely off my radar.

Now I am surrounded by people who like me just the way I am. And that's why I speak out about it. It just got to be too ridiculous. Especially for someone like me, who is here because I am a highly trained musician, not because I am just some pretty face trying to make it in the music business.

People often ask me in interviews why I didn't want to become a pop singer. I just tell them that I'm not here for that. I'm here because I'm a musician who spent all of my life thus far studying a certain kind of music, and that's what I want to give to the world. It's not because I want to "make it" and be a star. The whole thing is ridiculous!

If you were able, at this point in your life, to leave a note for your younger self when you were just starting out, what would the note say?

It would be a list of people to never get involved with—in business terms, not in romantic terms. (That, thankfully, I've always gotten right!) It would be a list of warnings. Basically, just a very, very strongly worded message to never let anyone push me around because I let it happen for way too long.

Do you have a favorite quote that inspires or motivates you?

I really don't have a quote that I live by.

What does music mean to you?

I don't even think I could put that into words because it's just like breathing. It's like air, or water, or sleep—it's just something that's required. It's a part of life. If it wasn't there, I think I would probably just be incredibly sad, incredibly depressed, and not realize why, at first. It has to be there, just like anything else that helps us survive.

Randy Brecker

✦

Birthdate: November 27, 1945

Birthplace: Philadelphia

Main instruments: Trumpet, flugelhorn

Other instruments: Piano, drums

Website: www.randybrecker.com

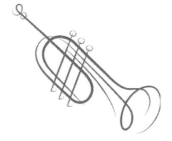

How long have you been a professional musician?

I started working in Philly, when I was around fifteen. I started to play around town with saxophonists like Lew Tabackin and Billy Root, and with Jimmy DePriest, who was a drummer and organizer. He became known as James DePriest, a very well-known classical conductor. But at the time, he was organizing youth bands, and he contacted Lew and me to play together.

Then I was also sitting in with another wonderful alto saxophonist whose name was Clarence "C" Sharpe. I also started doing dance gigs with a blues band. That was a little later because

RANDY'S MUSICAL NOTES

♪ Randy formed The Brecker Brothers, with his brother Michael, a saxophonist. Together, they recorded eight albums, including the double-Grammy winning *Out of the Loop* (GRP Records, 1994).

♪ As a solo artist, Randy has won four Grammy awards (1997, 2003, 2006, and 2008). In 2008, he also received the Edison Jazz Award, which is the Dutch award for outstanding achievement in music.

♪ The New York Chapter of the National Academy of Recording Arts and Sciences (NARAS) has honored him five times as "Most Valuable Trumpet Player."

♪ His musical family includes his wife, saxophonist Ada Rovatti Brecker, and daughters, vocalist Amanda, and budding vocalist Stella, age two-and-a-half.

I was driving by then. So I worked pretty extensively in Philly and also down the shore in Wildwood, backing up people like Al Martino and Bobby Rydell, and in Atlantic City doing the same thing.

Have you had to support yourself with other jobs, or has music been your only profession?

I was pretty lucky, early on, to be able to support myself just doing this. It's a combination of being in the right place at the right time, but also having material ready to record when opportunity knocked. One thing led to another; it's all been a pretty steady progression. I didn't have to work flipping burgers—at least not yet!

What drew you to playing the trumpet?

My father was a big jazz fan, and he loved trumpet players first and foremost. From my earliest recollections of consciousness, I heard trumpet players around my house, both live in jam sessions—he was also a piano player—and from his records. He had a great record collection of 78s and 10- and 12-inch LPs: Clifford Brown, Dizzy [Gillespie], Miles [Davis]—those were some of his favorites.

I started playing when I was eight, in the third grade at my school, which was outside of Philadelphia. They didn't have much of a music program. It was a small school, and they only had trumpets or clarinets available for study. I saw the trumpet and said, "Well, I know that instrument." So I grabbed it right away. I've been playing it ever since.

What drew you to jazz music?

It was the music that my father was interested in. His three kids all got interested early on. I remember even in the third grade, I loved jazz so much. Each week someone was chosen from the class to bring in their favorite record. This was in the heyday of Elvis Presley and the beginnings of rock and roll. All the eight-year-old kids were bringing in Elvis and Jerry Lee Lewis, and all the other stuff that was popular. I brought in a 45 by Lambert, Hendricks & Ross, with Jon Hendricks singing "Cloudburst." So I was already a hip eight-year-old kid.

Who played the most significant role in your musical development? Why?

My father pretty early on guided my brother [Michael Brecker] and me. My brother played the clarinet three years later because he didn't want to play the same instrument that I did. He went on to play the alto saxophone, then tenor and EWI [Electric Wind Instrument] and all the wonderful things that he did. We had a family band, and Mike and I doubled on drums and vibes. My sister played bass. There were jam sessions at the house all the time because my father liked to play on weekends, and he would have people over.

When I was fifteen, I met Evan Solot, who is a wonderful Philly trumpet player, arranger, and teacher who went on to head the University of the Arts music program. Tony Marchione, who was his teacher, became my teacher. Tony was a wonderful classical trumpet player, but he had one foot in jazz, too. He grew up with people like Lee Morgan and Benny Golson and a bunch of other guys who lived in Philly. Tony was actually Lee Morgan's trumpet teacher, and he became my teacher for five or six years until I went to college. He was a big influence.

Plus, just listening to records. I can't discount that, even though they weren't live influences. Miles Davis's records, and those by Shorty Rogers, Chet Baker, Dizzy Gillespie, Clifford Brown, Art Blakey—I could go on and on. I started playing along with records when I was about ten.

Is the life that you are living bigger than the one you had envisioned for yourself?

My main dream was to be a New York City freelance trumpet player. I never imagined the level of success that I've had throughout the years. With regard to live performances, I'd always thought that I would probably be a local trumpet player in New York and do Broadway shows and theater, and what have you. Somewhere along the line, I started to write music, almost thinking of it as a hobby, since I was doing a lot of sessions to make a living. I was playing a lot of live dates around town with various groups, among them the jazz-rock band Dreams. I also began writing my own music and eventually formed the Brecker Brothers.

What have you learned about your character as a result of being in this business?

It takes some strength and some fortitude, and, not in a bad way, aggressively pursuing your dreams. From knocking on doors and asking guys if you can sit in, to always trying to feel confident about your playing—which one does, if one stays in the practice room to learn new things and write new things. It is a constant battle and challenge to play music and remain relevant. So it does take some fortitude. I still practice. If I didn't practice, it would only take maybe three or four days before I wouldn't be able to get a sound out of the trumpet.

Was there anyone who said that you wouldn't be able to make it in the music business—what was your response to him or her?

My father had mixed feelings because it's an unstable lifestyle; but at the same time, we almost had no other choice because there was so much music in the family. Both my brother and I dabbled in and out of music school and the liberal arts. I remember I tried a semester in communications, and another semester in creative writing, but everything always fell back into music because that's what we did the best and loved the most.

Were there times when you thought that you might not make it yourself?

Not really. We all had concerns about some things, though. The old joke was two musicians meet in the street and one says, "Last week I won the lottery, thirty million dollars, and my aunt left me twenty million dollars. Terrible, terrible news." His friend says, "Well, you just got all that money, what do you have such a sad face about?" And the first guy says, "Well, this week I got nothing!"

That's how we musicians all feel, you know? We are always waiting for the phone to ring, or trying to figure out our next project. But I was pretty lucky in that I moved to New York at a very good time, when a lot was happening. It was before the advent of all the jazz education programs that brought thousands and thousands of musicians to New York. The fact that I was twenty-one and kind of knew how to play was kind of a novelty, so I got invited to play in a lot of circumstances.

When I arrived in New York, I was still known on the university circuit from doing college contests. One that I had won was the Notre Dame Jazz Festival, where Clark Terry was the judge. So when I arrived in New York, he called and invited me to join his big band. I had also met Mel Lewis at another competition in Vienna; he called too, and I joined the Thad Jones/Mel Lewis Orchestra. Then Horace Silver called. Duke Pearson, too. It was also around that same time that I was asked to join the original Blood, Sweat & Tears. Things picked up pretty quickly for me; I was very lucky in that regard.

What, for you, was the most unexpected aspect about being a professional musician?

Just how much work was available back then. There was a lot of studio work, and there were a lot of bands being formed. My dad had really cautioned me about how challenging it might be to make a living, but both my brother and I did quite well when we were young. We would bring the money home, and he would count it and be amazed by the amount! So that part was unexpected. Quite often it is very hard for a musician just starting out, especially these days because there are so many other players around. Studio work kind of folded up when the technology overtook the need to have live musicians around. So, things are a lot different now.

If you were able, at this point in your life, to leave a note for your younger self when you were just starting out, what would the note say?

Just believe in yourself and work on your voice. My advice to younger players is, whether you find your voice as a writer, composer, or player, always look for that thing that separates you from everyone else.

Do you have a favorite quote that inspires or motivates you?

A journalist in Germany once asked me, somewhat sardonically and sarcastically: "Is there any music you don't like?" But I always remember what Duke Ellington said, and I always took this to heart, "There are only two kinds of music: good and bad." So I don't really set boundaries on what I like, or what I listen to, stylistically.

What does music mean to you?

Music is my religion. It really is. It is all encompassing, along with my family. It is my life, my calling. I realize that now; I realized that a long time ago. It's exciting. I enjoy it.

Mark Small

✦

Birthdate: August 24, 1974

Birthplace: Norwalk, Connecticut

Main instrument: Tenor saxophone

Other instruments: Alto saxophone, soprano saxophone, clarinet, flute

Website: www.marksmallmusic.com

How long have you been a professional musician?

I got my first paying gig at fifteen or sixteen years old. It was playing at a birthday party with Eric Miller's quartet in Norwalk [Connecticut] when I was a sophomore in high school. I remember getting fifty dollars, which is funny because today most original music gigs in New York City at little jazz clubs still pay about fifty dollars.

I guess you could say I've been a professional since around 1990. It's hard to say when you cross the line, but I didn't get really serious until I went to college.

Have you had to support yourself with other jobs, or has music been your only profession?

I've been very fortunate in that, since high school, I have been able to support myself by doing something in the field of music, be it performing or teaching. I've been teaching privately since I was in college, and when I first moved to New

MARK'S MUSICAL NOTES

♪ Currently, Mark is pursuing his Doctor of Musical Arts degree at the University of Miami.

♪ He enjoys reading, especially books by David Foster Wallace and by Umberto Eco.

♪ When Mark was eight, he was a checkers champion for his hometown (Norwalk, Connecticut) Parks and Recreation.

♪ He has five siblings, almost all of whom played guitar at one point in their lives—yet he does not.

York City, I was traveling back and forth two days a week to teach at a college in Connecticut. I was also lucky that I moved to New York when I did because a lot of my friends moved around the same time, and I was able to find work through them. I would start each month off with a slightly empty calendar and think, "Will I make my rent this month?" And gradually, as the days went by, it would fill up. I would never really have much planned beyond a month or two. I can honestly say that I've lived in New York for ten years and always supported myself with music alone.

What drew you to the saxophone?

I wasn't actually drawn to the saxophone from the start. I had played violin in elementary school as a way of getting out of class and because it was fun. Admittedly, it wasn't the most sincere beginning.

When it came time to go to middle school, we could choose band instruments. Since a bunch of my friends chose the saxophone, I decided to go with that. It was putting in the work that I didn't like. I didn't really do that until I got to high school. Then I got serious about it. I had to make a choice about whether or not I was going to take it a little more seriously. But even then, I didn't plan on doing it as a profession.

During my sophomore year of high school, someone asked me to play at a party, and I had so much fun playing in a jazz band at a birthday party. Then I got paid! I didn't know I could have so much fun playing the saxophone with these guys who were older than I was—they were all seniors at the time. To get paid seemed completely unnecessary!

I always had wanted to go into science. I was going to do that, maybe physics. During high school, I went to the Manhattan School of Music Summer Jazz Workshop.

I think the moment that planted the seed for me to pursue

jazz music seriously was when I went to see the Vanguard band
[the Vanguard Jazz Orchestra]. I'd heard big band music before, and I thought it was good. I'd played a lot of it in high
school and middle school, and I didn't think anything of it.
Then I went to see this band, and I specifically remember
them playing, "Skylark." It's in *The Real Book,* the book of
jazz standards, which every jazz musician usually has. I thought,
"Oh, I know this song; I've played that before." But this arrangement by Bob Brookmeyer was so unlike anything I had
ever heard, it blew all my expectations out of the water! I had
no idea what to think. Then this alto saxophone jumped in,
with Dick Oatts playing this unbelievable solo. It was just the
most broad, beautiful music I'd ever heard. The fact that it was
a song that I thought I knew, with everything turned on its
head, made me realize I didn't know anything about this music.
These guys are *serious*!

Pretty much from that point on, I wanted to play with the
Vanguard band. The music that they have, the music that Thad
Jones has written—plus everyone who has worked for that
band—it's phenomenal music. I can't even think of a chart that
I don't like. I just loved that band so much, I started going to
see them pretty regularly. That was a big turning point, hearing
that. That made me want to play professionally, or at least play
in that band.

What drew you to jazz music?

In middle school, you could take saxophone lessons and
then play in concert band. Our music was okay, but playing
saxophone, you always got the big whole note, the most boring
parts. Flutes and clarinets were always doing all this fun stuff,
and saxophones didn't really do anything. So when I began
playing in jazz band in middle school, it was a lot more fun.
We played songs like "Tuxedo Junction" and such. It was just

this immediate draw—"Oh, that's what I want to do; I want to play in the jazz band." Then I started getting solos because it was so much easier for me to play by ear than to read music. I liked it, but I still hadn't listened to any real jazz music. I basically had just heard what we played.

In high school I had friends who listened to jazz, and I started borrowing and copying tapes. I remember one thing that intrigued me and made me want to learn more was a tape of Charlie Parker and Dizzy Gillespie. I don't remember the name of the album or anything like that, but it had "Groovin' High" on it. I remember hearing the trumpet, and I remember hearing the saxophone, but there was another instrument on it. I couldn't figure out what it was, but I kept singing along with it. It sounded like a comb with a piece of paper, that kind of harmonica-like buzz. It was really easy to sing along with. It was so melodic; I just didn't know what that instrument was, though. I found out later it was Slam Stewart playing arco bass and singing. He would bow, but he would sing along with his bowing. It was so perfectly in tune, that if you weren't seeing it live, you couldn't imagine that's what it was. I remember rewinding my tape over and over and singing those parts. To this day, I still can sing that solo. I think I'd have to credit him for my early enthusiasm for jazz.

I guess that was the first time—and I didn't even mean to—that I was transcribing, which a lot of jazz musicians do. You just sit down, and you learn a solo that somebody else plays, with the language, the notes, the articulation, the style, everything that they do, just so you can learn to play that style of solo with that same feeling. Some people don't agree with this. I've heard some jazz musicians say transcribing is not good because why would you want to learn to play like someone else? But I feel you can still be yourself even if you learn the "speech" of someone else. You can learn a Shakespeare monologue, but it doesn't mean you are going to walk around all day talking like that.

Who played the most significant role in your musical development? Why?

My first private teacher (I came to find out later) was loosing his eyesight, so he started me right in with improvising. He skipped right over any music I brought in from school to work on. It's no wonder I was the worst sax player in my lesson group as far as the book went, but I always got to play solos in the middle school jazz band.

I'd say my first long-term sax teacher in high school played a pretty significant role in my being a musician. I hear so many stories from other people who don't play anymore because when they started, their teacher was strict and unbending. They just weren't as into it as the teacher wanted. Now I see professional musicians who teach and complain that their students aren't serious. I was not serious when I started. I just wanted to do it for fun. My teacher, Steve Fasoli, made sure that I was enjoying the instrument while steering me in the right direction. He allowed me to come to the music at my pace and keep the joy that playing an instrument can give from the beginning, without beating it out of me. I may not be the Olympic athlete that some saxophone players are these days, but I do know where the joy in music is, and I try to express that with the tools that I have. I find that pretty significant.

The next person would be my teacher in college, Dave Santoro. He was able to show me a real method for learning how to apply the theoretical side of music to my playing so that I could incorporate it seamlessly. He could tell that I had a joy from the creative side, but not much of the theoretical or mathematical knowledge. He taught me how to connect the ear-type playing that I did with the brain. He showed me how you have to train some things into your ear that you might not be able to just intuit or hear right away. This helped me to see how I could make my practice work into my actual playing, rather than doing it in the practice room and not being able to bring it to the bandstand. Most teachers I had before that just gave me an idea of the knowledge and then said, "Well, now go practice." Without a method, it's just theory.

Is the life that you are living bigger than the one you had envisioned for yourself?

I actually didn't really start out with a vision of a career, so to speak. I knew I liked to play, and when someone actually handed me money for doing it, I think that's when I realized that I could do this forever. It only started to sink in later that there was music I didn't want to play because it didn't speak for me or for anything that I believed in.

It is my constant struggle, now, to find a way to play the music that speaks for me and says the things I want to say, and to balance that with making a living.

What have you learned about your character as a result of being in this business?

One thing that comes to mind is that I have a hard time being able to just kind of smile when somebody says something that is inappropriate, or that I don't agree with. To make it to the top of your field, you have to have the stomach for taking that kind of thing and not really acknowledging it. Smiling when somebody says something that is really inappropriate—I feel I can't do that. So I don't imagine that I would become a superstar. There would be someone along the way that I would just have to be honest with.

Being an improviser, I get to be honest while I am playing. I still get to be a character in a story, as well, but I get to play it the way I want to play it. In actual life, sometimes you can go really far by just being a character, knowing what people want to hear, and doing those things to advance your career. I just can't do that. I'd rather stay honest with how I feel and with the people that I want to play with and surround myself with. I know when to walk away from a situation if I can't smile and just nod my head and say yes to somebody.

But I've seen people who know how to kind of play things right go further faster. Yet, I feel that it comes out in the way they play music. Maybe people don't hear it. But hearing the music, I feel that it's in there; you can't hide your personality when you are playing. It kind of comes out, regardless. So a lot of times, I feel that if you listen to a good amount of what they play, you can really get a sense of the person.

I like the music, but I don't like the idea of the music business. I think I've known that for a long time, but it's one of those things that, with time, has been proven over and over. It's a lesson I continue to learn. Do the ends justify the means? I'm more about the in-between, and the journey itself being more important to me than just getting to a goal.

Was there anyone who said that you wouldn't be able to make it in the music business—what was your response to him or her?

My parents were always really supportive of whatever I decided to do. When it came to music, I think they were already seeing that the awards for soloing at jazz competitions, and such, were enough evidence to say that I had potential. With that, they had an attitude of, "What can we do to help?" That's why it's strange to me now to hear people say, "You really play music professionally?" I just didn't ever think that you couldn't, when I was growing up.

No one ever said to me that I wouldn't make it, but I will say that a few people tried to steer me towards a career in music education as a back up. I realized early in college that education is not a back-up plan; it's a calling. I loved teaching privately, one on one, which I still do. The type of education that you get in college for teaching, though, doesn't co-exist with being a full time player and realizing your potential in that respect. I have too much respect for the people who followed that path at University of Connecticut to have just tried to skim by on the education side while really applying myself to be a player.

Were there times when you thought that you might not make it yourself?

I never really doubted that I could make it as a professional musician. I guess that sounds funny to say now. Who knows—in a few years from now, maybe I won't be able to. It's a very different situation than just getting a job. I'm realizing that there is a real struggle between trying to stay true to a message that you want to send out through your music, a way of honestly connecting with people, and the flip side of just doing what people will pay you to do. If you do what people want, you can always make money. In that respect, there's always a way to get by. I would like to play music that comes from the heart. It takes time for people to really connect with something they're not familiar with, but I feel the end results are much deeper and make a real impact on their lives. Music can really change the way people think and feel, if it's honest. Hopefully, it will continue to support me while I pursue that.

What, for you, was the most unexpected aspect about being a professional musician?

I think because all of this stuff has happened so gradually, it hasn't felt so unexpected as it might have. Definitely, certain things just catch me off guard, and I am still just amazed by them when they happen—things that are bizarre and beautiful at the same time—like when I went to Bulgaria a couple of years ago. It was never like I thought, "Yeah, I really want to go to Bulgaria!" But it was such an amazing experience. It's not the kind of trip that you come back from and people are like, "So, how was Bulgaria?" Bulgaria is just different. It's post-Communist; it's gritty. But I enjoy it more, going somewhere where it's just a whole different experience and a different culture, than just going to the beach, you know? I mean, I love going to the beach, but to see something historic and catch a glimpse of something that's on its way out, or on its way in, is much more meaningful. The beach will still be there. It is pretty amazing to travel and see other cultures and be exposed to that.

But some interesting experiences are just sort of weird and quirky. I remember playing at The Town Hall with Michael [Bublé], and I knew that Liza Minnelli was there, but she left before the encore was over.

In New York, some of the theaters don't have the space to spread out. So, I am climbing the eight stories or whatever to get to the dressing room. As I'm going up the last steps, there's Liza Minnelli standing there. She said, "You were wonderful!" I just replied, "Oh, thanks."

I was really shocked! I had thought she had left. I didn't know that much about her, but I'd seen *Arthur*. She's part of that cultural consciousness that you know about, even if you don't know about her specifically. She's in *there*. So then she said, "I'm Liza." And all I could say to her was, "I know!" Those kinds of meetings are certainly unexpected.

If you were able, at this point in your life, to leave a note for your younger self when you were just starting out, what would the note say?

I guess the first thing that comes to mind is, "Don't wait to make a move on anything." Don't wait to be prepared, as much as to just go for it. There are certain opportunities that—I don't want to say I lost them—but I didn't wind up jumping on them. I definitely don't regret it, but I still wonder what would have happened. It's not like I wish my life had turned out differently—I don't. And if I changed anything, it would change everything. But if I had to say something to a younger self, it would be, "If you are thinking of doing anything, just do it, and see where it takes you."

Do you have a favorite quote that inspires or motivates you?

I don't have a specific quote, but I follow certain things about Taoist principles. One is just allowing the river to take you. You want to put in a little effort so you can stay above water, but you can just let the river take you. I feel it's kind of happened in my musical career a lot.

What does music mean to you?

It's an open canvas. It's like playing around when I was a little kid, and I got to make up stories, draw, and play, and how much fun that was. Even when it wasn't fun—being involved with winning and losing, and accomplishing something—it's still fun because it's creative. It's this constant construction and deconstruction.

John Patitucci

✦

Birthdate: December 22, 1959

Birthplace: Brooklyn

Main instruments: Acoustic Bass, Electric
Bass

Other instrument: Piano

Website: www.johnpatitucci.com

How long have you been a professional musician?

I used to play in rock-and-roll bands when I was twelve, and I was out playing gigs as a teenager. A gentleman named Vince Crudele, a wonderful jazz pianist, used to pick me up and drive me to gigs because I couldn't drive. I must have been about fourteen, fifteen years old. I started playing parties with other kids. In high school, I was doing some recording sessions for people. I worked a lot all through high school in my brother's band; we did a lot of gigs.

During college, I did a ton of live gigs and a lot more recording work, as well. Two years after I quit school, I moved to L.A. This was 1982, and I had already been driving down there doing a fair amount of work for a couple of years. So, I've been actively playing music professionally since I was a teenager.

Have you had to support yourself with other jobs, or has music been your only profession?

I've been doing music, and only recently have I supplemented that. Now I am also a university professor at City College in New York, in Harlem. I started teaching there around 2002, after Ron Carter, the famous bass player retired. I wanted to spend a little more time at home because I have two daughters and a wonderful wife. I don't want to travel as much as I have in years past. I've been on the road since I was nineteen, and I turned fifty in 2009.

I'm still doing a fair amount of traveling; it's inevitable. The university job provides great health benefits, a pension, and a really good investment plan. It helps me to be a little bit more choosy about who I'll go out of town with. I'm thankful, but you have to work really hard when you are self-employed. I write books, I teach, I do a lot of things to sort of put it all together so I can take care of my family.

Teaching has influenced my playing in many ways. You wind up accessing all this stuff in your memory banks from the music you studied throughout your life. Then there are the interpersonal relationships, and you learn a lot trying to reach everyone. Each kid is different. There are some generalities; certain groups learn better in some ways than in others. Certain things that came easily to me do not come easily for them. And some things come easily for them did not come easily for me. I'm constantly trying to find new ways to address and inspire my students with as much helpful information as possible.

JOHN'S MUSICAL NOTES

♪ John has won three Grammy Awards, in 1987, for Best R&B Instrumental Composition, with Chick Corea; in 1989, for Best Jazz Instrumental Performance, with the Chick Corea Acoustic Band; and in 2005, for Best Jazz Instrumental Album individual or Group, with the Wayne Shorter Quartet.

♪ In 1986, the National Academy of Recording Arts and Sciences (NARAS) voted him the Most Valuable Player on acoustic bass.

♪ One of John's childhood sports heroes was Leroy Kelly, a running back with the Cleveland Browns in the 1960s, who played alongside the famous Jim Brown. He loved to run and had dreams of being a running back, before he became immersed in the bass.

♪ John loves to cook, (and eat), especially his special ravioli con tre formaggi, a recipe handed down by his grandfather. He is also a self-claimed espresso fanatic.

I can also see a big difference in the generations now who are used to having everything thrown at them. They don't really have to reach for stuff that much. In a way it's good, and in a way it is very bad. We didn't have as many written materials available to us to help us learn how to play. And they do. Sometimes I think the students can become blasé because of that. Their work ethic is not the same, I would say, in general, as the work ethic I was forced to have. There are some great exceptions, and I have some students who are really fantastic. But then there are a lot of students who don't understand how much work is going to be required for this journey that they are embarking on.

You do learn a lot as a teacher. You learn a ton about how to reach people. You learn a lot about how to speak to people and try to motivate them. I also have a particular attitude about that. With music, if you have to spend too much time motivating the students, then it is time for them to get into another career.

You have to have passion. You play music because you are driven to do it, because you love it so much and you have such a passion for it. If you don't really have that, you are going to be in trouble because it's tough out there. This is a rough choice, especially in the world today. You want to be an artist? You want to be a musician? You'd better be passionate, and you'd better be dedicated spiritually to this path because it's a calling. It's not just something you dally with. You grab it and you run—as far as you can and as fast as you can. You work at it, and you put your whole soul into it. It's not, "Oh, I think I'll do this, this looks like fun." That's not what it is. And some people think that.

If I see that the students don't have passion for the music, then I really worry about them. I am not the kind of person who has ever told somebody, "You shouldn't do this." Because you don't know, actually. Somebody who seems improbable might have a cataclysmic event that inspires them, and they go crazy and practice ten hours a day for three years and all of a sudden emerge as an incredible musician. But usually in college, if they are in their twenties, and they haven't found the passion for music yet, it's not a great sign. Because it's hard out there.

In New York City alone, there are more incredible bass players than anywhere else in the world, in my opinion. They come here from all over the world. I try to tell the students, "Look, if you don't have the passion and real work ethic, and you don't want to work your tail off, there's a hundred other guys they can call." So you have to make a compelling case for yourself. And that's just the musical part of it. Then it's how you treat people, and how you make people feel when you show up. That's what makes people want to call you back. It's not good enough to be a really great musician but a drag to work with. That's a very complicated thing you have to teach. You have to teach life.

I enjoy teaching. I've really embraced it, and I take it really seriously. It's fun. I never wanted to be one of those guys that put their name on the brochure and have the kids think, "Oh, great, he's going to be there!" But then the guy is never there. I do some traveling, but I pay guys out of my own pocket, really great pros, to come in and work with them if I have to be out on the road. My private students never see another bass player but me. I make up my private lessons with them if I have to be away. If I accept them into my studio, then I am committed to them.

They take good care of me at the college, and I am thankful to have the position. I am a full professor with tenure, and I don't even have a college degree. They based this on my life performance. The precedent was set years ago by an incredible jazz pianist, who has since died, named Sir Rolland Hanna, who taught at one of the City University of New York colleges. He was a phenomenal pianist, a great musician. He didn't have a degree, either. Our forefathers were paving the way again, as they always do.

What drew you to the bass?

There was a lot of musicality in my family, although there weren't any professional musicians. No one was ever professional until my brother started playing, and then we got interested. My brother, Tom, is three years older than I am; he is a great musician and also a pastor. He started the ball rolling by taking guitar lessons.

I had always tried to be like him, so I started taking guitar lessons, too. But I am left-handed, and they didn't really have many leftie guitars around in those days. So I was very uncomfortable, plus you had to play with a pick, and I didn't really like it. His teacher was starting him right off reading music and doing the whole thing by the book. At eight years old, I was pretty impatient. I was already playing some percussion with bongos and maracas, and I was singing and playing along with the radio, all that sort of kiddie stuff.

We were all singing a lot around the house. My brother saw that I wanted to do something, and he figured out that electric bass might be a good thing for me because it was smaller. I could play with my fingers on my right hand, and not use a pick and be a little bit more comfortable. And it did work; I played that and kept singing. I still fooled around with percussion and wanted to play the drums. By the time I was ten, I was playing electric bass at home and snare drum in the school band. I tried to get my dad to let me have a drum set, but he said no.

Later on, at thirteen years old, when we moved to Northern California, I encountered a man who became my mentor, Chris Poehler. He taught me to read music and introduced me to jazz, though I had heard some jazz records before that my grandfather brought home. That was amazing, but we didn't understand any of it. We couldn't even imagine what any of it was, but we started listening. It took us awhile, but we got interested through Wes Montgomery's, Art Blakey's, and Jimmy Smith's records.

I was about fifteen before I got my hands on an acoustic bass. The smaller kiddie versions didn't exist. Then, it took me awhile to be able to grow into holding one. Once I started acoustic bass, I kept practicing a lot on both. I did three years in college as a classical double-bass major. I was playing jazz and all kinds of music through my school years from junior high on, and I just kept going. I was very thankful and fortunate that God allowed me to pursue my dreams.

In 2007, I finally got to play a bass concerto in front of an orchestra. The piece was written for me by Mark Anthony Turnage. That was an incredible experience because they don't program bass concertos that much. A friend, Edgar Meyer, who is very well-known as a bass soloist around the world, does these things.

But the level of playing in the concerto world, and in the classical world, has gone berserk. All of the young guys are incredible. The level is very high, but the opportunity to go out and play solos with orchestras is very limited. The orchestra is going to program a season with a violin soloist, a piano soloist, maybe a cello concerto—but not so many bass concertos. It's not as common. So that was a big deal for me. I did eight performances of this concerto all over the world, the last three of which were with the St. Louis Symphony with David Robertson conducting. That was amazing fun and very scary at the same time.

What drew you to jazz music?

The very first music that got me interested in the bass, since I also was into the drums, was from Africa. First it was R&B, and blues, and stuff that I heard on the radio. Then it became jazz in all its forms, including what is called Latin Jazz, a very nebulous term. Basically, African music influenced South American music, as well, be it Brazilian, Peruvian, Cuban or

Panamanian. All of that became interesting to me. Early on, I had sort of an open mind, and I liked a lot of different things. Of course, I was also into the classic rock because I was born in 1959. The British Invasion, The Beatles, Cream, the Rolling Stones, etc.—plus Jimi Hendrix—all that stuff influenced me. I had three years of classical bass lessons in college, and then I just left school and went on the road. My classical teachers were shocked and very unhappy. I loved classical music too, so they assumed that I was just going to be an orchestral bass player. (And not "just" because that's an incredible job, and you have to be a great musician to be able to do that.)

I loved that, but I loved all this other music too, so it was kind of difficult for me to stay within their parameters. The way my teachers were presenting it to me, which is another reason why I made the choice I made, was that it was all, or nothing at all. You do this orchestral thing, and you don't do the other things. Or, you do these things for a while, and maybe years down the road you can go experiment with your jazz thing, as if it were a dalliance. That wasn't sitting well with me, so I folded.

Ironically, now I am playing tons of classical music, more than I ever have, especially chamber music, and I compose it, too. I do love orchestral music and the feeling of playing with other bass players, which I don't get to do that often except when we play orchestral music for films. But I love that sound, playing with seven other guys, or whatever. The sound of a bass section is really beautiful. While I don't get to do as much, I am getting to do so many other things. That's the way it goes. You can only be in one place at one time.

Who played the most significant role in your musical development? Why?

My brother, Thomas, has always been a teacher and a major inspiration in my life. After him, Chris Poehler, a great bassist, composer and arranger, has been a consistent mentor to me since I was thirteen years old. I had some other very important bass teachers, such as Charles Siani. He is no longer with us, but Charles was the principal bass player of the San Francisco Opera. I had Abe Luboff as a teacher for two years, and he had a big impact on me. In more recent years, in my classical studies, I would say John Schaeffer and Tom Martin have been teachers who helped me enormously.

Tom Martin was very influential because I did a record many years ago called *Heart of the Bass* [Stretch Records, 1997]. It was one of my forays into the mixture of jazz and classical music as an adult, after I already had established myself making records as a bass player, bandleader, and composer. It was a pretty miraculous thing for me, that I got to make records. I didn't really assume that I'd get to do all that. *Heart of the Bass* was my fifth or sixth record. I did some music with the orchestra, and some different kinds of things. I played some with the bow; I also played my six-string electric bass. Then I got a letter from Tom Martin, principal bassist of the London Symphony Orchestra. I opened the letter thinking, "Oh no! He heard my record. He must hate it!" Quite the contrary; he said, "Great record, I loved it! You should do more music like this. Obviously you have a heart for this."

So we started corresponding, and he sent me the music of [Giovanni] Bottesini, who was a famous double bassist in Italy and a true virtuoso of the instrument. He was one of the two main virtuosos in the history of Italian bass playing, which has quite a long history, pedagogically, in all sorts of classical music. (By the way, I happen to have the same birthday as Bottesini—December 22.)

Tom said, "You're Italian; you should be playing Bottesini's music." Tom is an expert on that music, so he started sending the music to me, and I started practicing it more and more. He would give me pointers, and when I made it to London, he would show me some stuff. He has been to my house, and we worked on some bowing exercises. He's just a great guy, a true bass virtuoso, and a great musician. He's helped me a lot.

When I came to New York, I said I really want to work on my bowing and get my classical playing stronger. I asked Tom, "Who would you send me to, if you knew someone who wanted to work with me?" And he said, "John Schaeffer." He didn't even hesitate.

So I studied with Schaeffer from 1996 to 1998, and he had a big impact on my playing. He was a very fine teacher, and he used to be principal bassist of the New York Philharmonic. He was very organized and very picky. He didn't really care about people's reputations and was not that aware of my career, which was great. He just said, "No, you need to do this, this, and this." At first, when I played for him, he said, "I don't want to change a lot of stuff. You've been playing for years."

I told him, "No, I came to you because I want you to tell me anything and everything you're thinking."

So he said, "Well, okay, this is how I do it." He actually changed my grip of the bow a bit and gave me lots of stuff to practice. He was great because he kind of tortured me for a couple of years and gave me all this stuff to work on. It was really good for me. I felt I really was able to improve, utilizing all the things that we were working on. That was ultimately really enjoyable, and I continue to think about those things.

Jazz-wise, a whole bunch of people influenced me. David Baker is an incredible musician who has been teaching at Indiana University for years. He pioneered a lot of things, and he worked himself through college and got advanced degrees. He went from being an incredible jazz musician, steeped in the tradition, to becoming the godfather of jazz education in America. He taught people how to teach jazz.

He gave me some ear training when I was in high school and spent a couple of weeks at jazz camp with him. When I took my entrance exams for classical studies at San Francisco

State University, I tested out of ear training and never had to take it because David Baker had had us doing really heavy ear training. I still stay in touch with him, and he's a really great guy, as well.

Among the musicians that I've worked with, some of the biggest influences are: Wayne Shorter, who I still work with and have since 1986, on and off; Chick Corea, who I was with for ten years and still play with here and there; and Herbie Hancock, who I still play with from time to time. Those guys were huge influences on me, and still are.

Is the life that you are living bigger than the one you had envisioned for yourself?

Oh, sure. You have no idea, when you are twelve, like I was, when I decided I wanted to be a musician for the rest of my life, how that would look, frankly. I didn't know the half of it. I was so naïve, I didn't even know how hard it was. I just thought, well, this is what I'm dreaming of, and this is what I'm going for. I had no idea how reckless a decision that could be. I thank God that He allowed me to pursue it.

I give a lot of credit to my parents because they didn't discourage me, even though they probably never thought I would be a musician. They didn't say, "No, you can't do that." They came to all the concerts. They had to go to a lot of concerts because everybody in my family wound up playing an instrument, singing, or doing both. They had five kids, and everybody was doing something. I guess they felt it was a good thing because they came out of a European culture. My parents were born here, but my father's father was straight from Italy. That kind of thing carried over—love and appreciation for music. So whether they thought anything was going to come of it professionally or not, and obviously they didn't, they thought it was good that we were involved in music. They didn't say, "Well, you can't do that, or don't do that." Nobody ever said that to me. I know other people whose parents said, "You can't do that. You have to be a doctor, or a lawyer, or this, or that, or anything except an artist of any kind."

What have you learned about your character as a result of being in this business?

For me, the most important things that I have learned about my character have come through my faith. But you do learn, as a musician, what your character is because the world of music is so competitive. And if you are not careful, you can wind up posturing, and comparing yourself to other people, and being critical of others. When you are a little insecure, like many of us artists tend to be, it is easy to try to feel better by being critical of others. It is wasted energy, and it can be very negative.

It can also be a self-centered environment among artists because they are trying to assert a point of view, a direction, and to express themselves. I think the important thing never to lose, as an artist, is to nurture each other in a community; it's always the best thing. You can still be striving like crazy for what you want to say and do as an artist, but you don't have to engage in that critical sort of stuff. But that's hard to learn, and it takes years. It's an issue of spirituality and maturity. It's easy, sometimes, to engage in negativity without even realizing you're doing it because the tendency is to compare and contrast.

When I first went to college, I didn't have as much experience as an orchestral musician, so I sat basically in the last stand of the bass section. I wasn't the absolute last guy, but I was down there. If I had let that deter me, it would have been very destructive. So I didn't. I just saw it as, "Well, I'm going to have to work to catch up to these other guys." And that's what I tried to do. The competitive thing has to be viewed healthfully, but it's usually not. People tear themselves down and beat themselves up because they can't do what so and so does, instead of trying to become the best version of who they are.

A healthy motivation can happen when you hear other people play. When I hear someone really playing, I sometimes get mad because it's so good! I'm like, "Oh, that drives me nuts—he's too good!" Usually it motivates me because it makes me think, "Wow! Listen to that!" It makes me think, "Oh, I should work on this." If you use competition as a positive thing, as a motivating thing, it's much more healthy. That takes a while to cultivate. You are putting yourself out there, and who you are should come through in your playing. It should be expressed quite openly. That's the goal of an artist—to be transparent and to really be saying who you are when you play. Some people are afraid of being rejected or not accepted for who they are. It's complicated, but it's exciting at the same time. I love it—most of the time!

I think certain kinds of character traits match the instrument that you play. On bass, you are supposed to be really supportive, and you are supposed to be good at making people sound good. That's your gig. It has evolved into a solo role over the years, in certain respects. But then there's still the basic thing that you get called to do—to be a catalyst and make people sound really great. You are there to thread needles and make stuff happen from the bottom. I like that. I like making people feel open. The biggest compliment I can get is for somebody to say, "Wow, I feel like I can play better, when I play with you. I feel more comfortable, and that I can get to stuff easier." That's great. People feel freer creatively and artistically, and that's what we like to hear as bass players.

And then, of course, we want to be ready if somebody wants to open up some space and says, "We really want you to step forward in this section, or play a solo." My whole thing growing up, was that I wanted to be able to make a contribution that way. I didn't like it when I heard groups with stellar soloists up front that would give the bass player a solo, and it would be like nothing happening for a minute or two. He really wasn't contributing in that way, but was sort of filling space. I didn't like that, so I didn't want to be like that.

Obviously, some big heroes in the history of the music showed that the bass could also be a virtuoso instrument. In jazz, people like Oscar Pettiford, Ray Brown, and Paul Chambers. Then afterwards, you had people like Ron Carter. There were a lot of guys who showed the bass has a lot of possibilities.

Was there anyone who said that you wouldn't be able to make it in the music business—what was your response to him or her?

Nobody ever discouraged me and said, "You'll never be able to do that." I also know some people were probably surprised, later on, that I was successful. There are some people who, for whatever reason, just didn't see anything in me. Sometimes it's because they are not sensitive to seeing that someone really has potential. Sometimes it's because, in their subjective viewpoint, they think, "Well, this guy is okay, but he is never really going to go places."

Nobody ever said it to me openly, but I have a feeling they were pretty surprised later because they hadn't heard me for about twenty years. Then they went, "Wow, look at this guy. He did turn into something!"

The gift is a huge part of it to me because I am a person of faith. I believe in God's input and His gift. I've known other guys who kind of wanted to be musicians, but that wasn't their gift. So they worked very, very hard and were never able to do it because they happened to be really good in something else, which they were ignoring. They were incredible at something else, but they would say, "I don't care about that. I want to play." Well, it didn't work out because they were supposed to be doing that other thing that they were so good at.

My parents didn't even entertain the idea that I could be a success as a professional musician; it was not even on their radar. It was like, "That's not a possibility; that's not going to happen for our son." Later on, when things did go well for me, I asked my dad, "What did you think I was going to do with my life?"

He said, "Well, I thought you'd be a salesman."

Were there times when you thought that you might not make it yourself?

I don't really think so. I think I was kind of naïve enough to have these dreams. I dreamed and kept practicing. I had this very naïve thing inside of me that said, "Well, if I work hard enough, it could happen," because I felt like it was something I was born to do. After a while, people would react in certain ways, and some people were encouraging me. It felt like, this is what I'm supposed to do. I don't think I really understood how reckless and insane it was until later on, when it all worked out. Then I looked back as an adult and thought, "Wow, what did I do? What happened? This could have really not worked, you know?" You don't really understand it fully until you get older. I think it was better that way, at least in my case. Otherwise, I would have been paralyzed by fear.

What, for you, was the most unexpected aspect about being a professional musician?

I guess it was when, all of a sudden, my dreams started to come true, and I found myself on the stage with Chick Corea, or Herbie [Hancock] or Wayne [Shorter]. I was used to buying their records and going to concerts, and all of a sudden, they are sitting right there: There they are, and it's happening—for real. That was always unexpected. Even in more recent years, every once in a while, I think, "Wow, this in incredible!"

I remember hearing Wayne when I was eight, on the first batch of jazz records that I got. I heard him play with Art Blakey and the Jazz Messengers. It was a big deal. Then all of sudden, there he is. I'm standing with him, and we've become really good friends.

And Chick. I'd spent ten years solidly with him at one point, and toured all over the world. That was the guy who got me my first record contract, and all that. It was unbelievable. My brother and I used to get his records, and here he was, helping me. He went to bat for me, I remember very clearly, in the eighties. A saxophone player in the band, a good friend of mine, was trying to get a record deal. The record company was very interested in him because he was great and he played the saxophone. They weren't so interested in me because I played the bass. They said, "Well, what are we going to do with a bass player?"

Chick told them, "If you are going to sign the saxophone player, then you've also got to sign the bass player."

They said, "Okay, we want to hear demos of his music."

Chick said, "No, you'll hear the record when it's done. He can compose, and I believe he's going to make a really great record. So just wait. When it is done, you'll hear it, and it will be great."

Chick sort of bought me artistic freedom for my first record. That's a huge gift to give somebody. He helped me to produce the first one, and after that, I produced them on my own. He instilled in me this confidence in my own direction so that even when the president of the record company, after that first record, was trying to make suggestions, or edit out certain things, I just said, "No, I don't want to do that." I don't know how I was able to say that to him, and I don't know why I told him that. I was a cheeky little guy, maybe too reckless and stubborn. Again, I think that was partially from being naïve because I felt so protected in that bubble, having Chick there. Once I believed something artistically, it was hard to shake me from sticking to a conviction. That's the way I am; I'm stubborn. If I really believe in something, it doesn't matter about money; it doesn't matter about anything. It only matters about the music and the art.

My dad used to laugh at my brother and me when we were kids. He'd say, "You guys, you think you'll never compromise. But you will." Sometimes I think I did, in certain ways, but never in big ways. Never when it came down to it. Even if it was a record company president saying, "You know, you should cut that out. That doesn't work." And I would say, "No. I can't do that."

That's probably why I never became a film composer. It would be difficult for me to listen to a music supervisor, who doesn't know anything about music, tell me how to re-write an entire orchestral piece, even if it is only one minute long. Somebody who doesn't know what they are doing telling you to rewrite something—that would be hard to accept. Some people might think that is a stubborn kind of pseudo-integrity, and not worth much. It makes you a lot less money in the long run, too. But for me, it's super important because I believe that if you are true to those kinds of ideals, and, if you do put integrity on the top of your list, and you try to be as truthful as you can be, as well as vulnerable and transparent, people will receive that music because it's genuine. Ultimately, you may not make the same kind of living as popularizers and people who seem to adjust everything they can, in order to make as much money as they can, but I'm not really interested in any of that. Otherwise, I wouldn't have gotten into the types of music that I love to play.

If you were able, at this point in your life, to leave a note for your younger self when you were just starting out, what would the note say?

I would say, pay more attention to your gut, and when God tells you to do something, just do it. And don't think that you're wiser than the years that you have. Because I learned some hard lessons that way, early on, when I was in a hurry to grow up. Later on, I learned you should never be in a hurry to grow up. You're going to grow up plenty fast. So that's what I would say. Otherwise, I would not change much because it came out way better than I ever expected.

Do you have a favorite quote that inspires or motivates you?

I've always been a big fan of Bach. He used to write on all of his scores, "Every note for the glory of God." Even if you are not a person who is very specific about what you believe (I happen to be, but I don't expect everybody to be of the same mind), you are aiming pretty high if every note that you are writing, and everything that you are trying to do with your music, is supposed to evoke a beauty and a presence that big.

What does music mean to you?

I don't think I could accurately say what music means to me, but I can say a couple of things. I think music is an incredibly powerful, spiritual thing that can motivate people and can change their lives. Some people feel that, and I agree, music also can heal people. It can make a real difference in people's physical, mental, and emotional well-being. I think it's one of the things that God values very highly because it can be a very encouraging, uplifting force in this world.

Wayne Shorter is an interesting man; he is a Buddhist, in fact. We talk a lot about being able to just "get" to people and encourage them. Because a lot of times, if a group is really playing together and really sharing, people feel that in the concerts. It shows them something. In a way, when music is working well, and people are really vulnerable and giving of themselves in a selfless, group-oriented expression, it's a microcosm of what society could be, if people were willing to think about community and the group, as opposed to bowing down to the almighty individual, which is what happens too often and is the source of a lot of problems in the world.

So that's what I think about music. It's way more than just my passion for playing. It's a beautiful part of the culture and an important part of the world. It's a thing that can create change, positive change.

Benny Green

✦

Birthdate: April 4, 1963

Birthplace: New York City

Main instrument: Piano

Website: www.bennygreenmusic.com

How long have you been a professional musician?

The first time I was paid, I believe I was fourteen; certainly it was by the time I was fifteen. I was playing in an R&B group with contemporaries of mine. There was a sax player by the name of Eddie Mininfield here in Berkeley [California], and Eddie was a really good player. I played Fender Rhodes electric piano. Was there a bass? Bass players were a rare commodity among our age group. There was the drummer and certainly a guitar. We played Parliament-Funkadelic kind of stuff for kids to dance to.

I got twenty dollars, and I don't think I'd even held a twenty-dollar bill before. It was a big deal, but mostly it was just exciting to play for the kids and to play that music.

BENNY'S MUSICAL NOTES

♪ Benny is the only pianist, other than Count Basie, whom Oscar Peterson chose to record with, which he did on two occasions.

♪ His favorite records to listen to, and learn from, are quintets with trumpet and saxophone made on the Blue Note label in the 1950s to 1960s by artists such as Hank Mobley, Lee Morgan, Jackie McLean, Art Blakey, and others.

♪ His hobby is collecting and watching old black-and-white Hollywood films, particularly film noir from the 1940s and 1950s.

♪ After many years of focusing his performance repertoire on jazz standards, he is reconnecting with his passion for writing music.

Have you had to support yourself with other jobs, or has music been your only profession?

Music has been my only profession, I am grateful to say.

What drew you to playing the piano?

We got a piano when I was six. My parents did not have a lot of money when I was growing up. They were both born in the late 1920s, grew up in the Depression, and there was just a basic family value that you had a piano in your home. I remember the day, it was raining and we went to a sort of used-piano warehouse in Oakland. My parents were choosing one, and, I believe, they were looking at the wood, as well as the quality of the keys and the sound they produced. I've asked my parents about it many times since. They did not have any intention of my sister or me specifically becoming musicians. They just thought, like reading books to us, that it was part of a healthy, well-rounded household and childhood to have a piano in the house.

I was completely fascinated with the instrument from day one, maybe not in an atypical way for a youngster. It was the fact that a sound could be produced without my having had any lessons. I could touch the keys and instantly hear a sound. Like most kids would notice, I noticed that I could choose low notes or high notes. It was like a whole new world, and I escaped into it. I started trying to write my own songs. I hadn't had any lessons; I didn't know anything.

I found a cigarette burn on the wood that marked the middle E, and I noticed the interval of a tenth going down to C, an octave below middle C. That C and the E were so resonant, that tenth. I would go to the piano and just diatonically go down with those tenths and play this rhythm, all the way down to the bottom and back up. I must have driven my parents crazy! It wasn't until years later that I realized it was

Beethoven. So probably I had heard it somewhere, in a cartoon or something.

My sister Phoebe is four years older than I am, and she started taking lessons around that time. So she must have been about ten. I asked my parents for lessons, and of course, my sister and I were very competitive with each other. She would be practicing her lessons, and I would be playing my little simple pieces that I was coming up with. Because we didn't have a lot of money, and because I was that young, my parents were unsure it would be a wise investment. But they saw after a year went by, by the time I turned seven, that I was still really hanging out with that piano and still asking for lessons. So they got me my first teacher around then. I wouldn't call them classical lessons so much as just children's introductory lessons to the piano: learning the names of the keys, fundamentals of reading music, and starting to play some simple nursery rhyme-type pieces. But the teacher noticed early on that I liked to vary the pieces each time. I thought, in her eyes, that was a bad thing, somehow—that I was changing them. But she actually telephoned my parents and said, "I think you should try and find a jazz teacher for Benny because he seems to like to improvise." She set me free in so doing.

What drew you to jazz music?

My father played the tenor saxophone, and he would play at home by himself. His primary influence was Lester Young, but he loved a lot of tenor saxophonists. He loved Dexter Gordon, who he used to take me to hear in the 1970s here in the San Francisco Bay area. He loved Gene Ammons. We would listen to Gene Ammons records together. But my father loved any tenor player that could play. So he loved Hank Mobley and [John] Coltrane. He loved Joe Henderson. My father really liked anyone that can play, but Prez (Lester Young), was his number one.

My father was a semi-professional player, but he didn't read music well. When he saw my interest in music, he encouraged me to learn to read music. He said that it had held him back, in terms of having a career. The first time I was on a record gig, many years later, I was giving thanks to my father silently for encouraging that. I had to read music and I was able to. My father had instilled it in me to make a priority of it.

My father was listening to records as well as playing his saxophone. The main record that he played so often around the house, which has really always been my foundation for the feeling of this music, is a Thelonious Monk LP called *Monk's Dream* [Columbia Records, 1963]. My father listened to this record, and I could discern, even as a young person, say five years old, that there were four instruments being played by four people. I could tell there was a saxophone and that it was the same instrument that my father played. I could tell there were a piano and bass and drums.

I felt the humanity in the music. My father would put the LP on in the back of our garage, where he would be sculpting. It was *magic*—the sounds produced by these humans would go through the air, into my father's ears, and I would see him smiling and start moving his body. I was *fascinated* with that energetic exchange. Without being able to put any words to it as a kid, I knew it was magical. We didn't have an instrument yet; we hadn't got our piano yet. But I can honestly say that was my foundation of wanting to be a musician—wanting to do *that.*

Who played the most significant role in your musical development? Why?

I studied jazz in my childhood, going into my teens, with several Bay area jazz pianists, all of whom helped me in unique ways and tremendously so. My first jazz teacher was a man named Dick Whittington, who some people will remember from the Maybeck Recital Hall Series recordings on the Concord label, which came years later. But at the time, he was actually teaching general curriculum at Longfellow Elementary here in Berkeley.

We had the benefit in all of the Berkeley elementary schools of a man who passed some years ago, Phil Hardymon, who would go from school to school beginning at the fourth-grade level, all the way up through high school, on a daily basis, and coach little jazz ensembles. So the goal, if you were in elementary school and interested, would be that when you got big you got to play in the high school jazz band, which was really something. That would be the equivalent of getting to play with Miles [Davis], you know? Phil helped us so much, and I didn't know that other cities, other kids, didn't have this opportunity. It was amazing.

Other teachers, after Dick Whittington, included a man named Carl Andrews. He helped me so much. I got a little more into harmony with him, learning to read chord symbols and to read a lead sheet out of a fake book, things like that.

Some other pianists that helped me out in the Bay Area were Ed Kelly and Bill Bell. And then there was Smith Dobson. He was wonderful, and I remember he took to me to a great club in San Francisco, which is now defunct, called the Keystone Korner. He took me to hear Horace Silver; this was back in the mid-to-late 1970s. He looked out for me. All these guys were looking out for me. Even though I was a little kid, they were treating me as a serious jazz student. I'm grateful for that.

I was born in New York City, and we moved to Berkeley when I was quite young. But before I moved back to New York, which I did for the music, I started working around the Bay Area on a regular basis, first with a singer named Faye Carroll. She helped me so much because on her gigs there was a real professional environment. I'd wear a suit and a tie. We would play standards and blues. We would begin the shows by my playing a trio tune or two. It was a serious training ground for me, as you could imagine. I was sixteen when I started with her.

Then I used to go around to jam sessions in the Bay Area and listen to jazz. There was a horn player that I really saw as a link to the East Coast guys and the guys that I would listen to on the records. His name was Eddie Henderson. This man had hung out and practiced with Lee Morgan and Freddie Hubbard, and he was a nephew of Miles Davis. Miles would stay at his family's home when Miles was in San Francisco. So this guy really knew what was up. I would go hear him play; I sat in with him, and eventually he hired me. I became a member of his group here in the Bay Area. He talked to me about New York and about the musicians I was curious about. He helped me so much, as did a man who was playing tenor with him, who just passed recently, Hadley Caliman. They both helped me so much.

When I was nineteen, it had become increasingly clear to me that New York was the place I not only wanted, but needed, to be, to groom myself as a jazz musician. I had a very specific goal. I had heard Art Blakey and the Jazz Messengers in person at the Keystone Korner. Everything clicked for me when I saw and heard the band. I actually visualized myself being on the bandstand playing for Art. I could see it, and I wanted to do that. Art would just lock his eyes in on the piano player and connect with him. I wanted to be that guy.

So when I moved to New York at nineteen, I had it in mind that I was going to go hear Art Blakey and the Jazz Messengers as much as possible, learn their repertoire, and really try and get it together musically so that I could be a Jazz Messenger one day.

When I was living in California, I had listened to Walter Bishop, Jr. on records with Jackie McLean, Miles Davis, and

Charlie Parker. Walter's nickname was "Bish." I really saw Bish as a link to these greats, to Bud Powell and this tradition of the music—bebop.

Shortly after moving to New York, I went to a gig where Walter was playing, called the Jazz Forum which has since closed. Walter was playing in a quintet co-led by Bill Hardman and Junior Cook. I shyly approached Walter on the intermission and asked him if he taught lessons. He told me that he did, and he gave me his card. I called him up and made an appointment. When I went to his apartment, he showed me a piano, went over to the window, lit up a cigarette, and just sort of gestured and said, "Play something." I played, as best I could, my simplified rendition of one of his arrangements that I had heard on a record. It was a trio arrangement of "Don't Blame Me" on a Jackie McLean album called *Capuchin Swing* [Blue Note Records, 1960]. As soon as I started to play, he came over, took the cigarette out of his mouth and said, "That's...." I said, "I know!" and we sort of bonded right then and there.

I came a week later for the second lesson. At the end of the lesson, I went to pay him, and he pushed my hand away and said, "Let's not keep it on this level." Now, as a nineteen-year-old, I didn't know what the heck that even meant! I held the money out again. This time he raised his voice, "I said, let's not keep it on that level."

That's when our friendship really began. He looked out for me so much. He was so much more real with me than simply being complimentary. He had been enthusiastic about my interest in real jazz, but he'd only heard me playing at home. He finally heard me playing a jam session, accompanying the horn, which he'd never heard before. After I finished, he said with a smile, "Can we step outside for a second?"

I said, "Sure." With my little kid's ego—I was so used to getting pats on the back from older people saying, "How old are you, kid?"—I just knew that he was going to compliment me.

We stepped outside, and he said, "What were you doing?"
I said, "What do you mean?"

He said, "You sound like a striped tie on a plaid shirt—way too busy! I can see we are going to have to work on your comping." And that was a lot of love. Anyone can pat you on the back, but he really cared. He really cared. He saw the first of many holes in my budding musicianship and cared enough to address it. I am so thankful to him for that.

Another man by the name of Walter, a great pianist named Walter Davis, Jr., also began helping me. I started studying with him because I was fascinated with his clear affinity for Thelonious Monk and Bud Powell. Thelonious Monk was my whole introduction not only to jazz but also to music itself. I heard it and felt it in Walter Davis Jr.'s playing. He helped me a whole lot. So that first year in New York, I would go to hear the Jazz Messengers as much as possible. I'd sneak my little Walkman tape recorder into the shows and record them, and then go home and practice the songs.

My friend John Donnelly, who is a bassist, had moved to New York with me in the spring of 1982. He drove us across the country in his Volkswagen bus. We both began playing for the Tuesday night jam session at the Jazz Forum, which was led by Jo Jones, Jr., the drummer. I got to meet a lot of people at the jam sessions because a lot of people would come through the Jazz Forum. It was located at Broadway and Bleeker [Street]. Art Blakey actually lived right around the corner, downstairs in a building called the Bleeker Court. Wynton and Branford Marsalis were living in the building at that time, as well. So Art would come to the Jazz Forum and hang out.

I got to meet Art's pianist at the time, a wonderful man named Johnny O'Neal. Johnny actually asked me early on in our friendship, "Do you think you'd like to play with Art one day?"

I said, "I really do."

"I'm going to introduce you to Art," he said. "I'm not going to be doing this forever."

So when Johnny finally introduced me to Art at the bar at the Jazz Forum, Art looked me up and down, literally from head to toe, and said, "How long you been in town?"

I said, "Six weeks."

He said, "You need more time." And he hadn't heard me play one note! He just read me. I later learned an expression Art was fond of saying, which was, "See with your ears and hear with your eyes." So I felt like he "heard" me. He could see how green I was, with my blue jeans and sneakers and plaid flannel work shirt, with all my enthusiasm.

I get it more than ever, now. As musicians, you can pretty much hear the way someone plays when you first meet them, just when you make eye contact. It's just something that happens over time, through experience. And yet, you don't want to make assumptions. You can certainly clearly see if a person has humility; that's very apparent.

One thing I noticed as soon as I moved to New York as a youngster, was that the older musicians, the masters, had a lot of brotherly love for young people if their heart and their ego were in a good place. They would open up; they wanted to share the music. They wanted to pass it on, which I understand more now than I did before, having lost some dear friends in music over the last few years. People who have passed on were bandleaders, mentors, and teachers of mine. They were just in life for a moment. You want to pass the music on to someone who will try to uphold the traditions of this music with honor and humility. I'm very, very thankful to the people who were looking out for me, and who continue to do so. And I try to do likewise.

So in either January or February 1983, the Jazz Messengers were playing at the Blue Note. I was down there hanging out and listening to them, and Johnny O'Neal came over and said, "Art said you can sit in tonight." What I did have going for myself was that I knew all their tunes. I wasn't a very experienced player, but I did know the book, which was a good thing, because when I got up there, Johnny whispered in my ear, "Ms. B.C." That was an original written by Bobby Watson's wife, Pamela, dedicated to Betty Carter (whom, little did I know, I was about to start working for a few months later). I knew the song; I definitely knew it. It was from a record called *Album of the Year* [Timeless, 1982] with James Williams playing piano. I'd been practicing it every day. So what made an impact, probably more than my playing itself, was that when Art played the introduction in time for the rest of the rhythm section to come in, for the piano and bass to enter, I knew what to do right there.

We finished the tune, and Johnny O'Neal came back to the piano. After the set, Art actually called me over and said, "Keep doing what you're doing. I'm gonna need you one day," which was exactly what I needed to hear. That gave me all the encouragement I needed. I felt like I was already a Messenger just from his saying he might need me one day. I felt like I was in line to play with him, which was why I had moved to New York in the first place.

So I was playing with a singer at a club on Long Island, called Sonny's Place, which is closed now. On the intermission, someone came in and mentioned that Betty Carter was in the audience. I was terrified! I just hid out and stayed in the dressing room the whole intermission. When it was time to start the second set, I took a few steps up to the stage, and as I was walking, someone tapped me on my back. I turned around and it was Betty. She said, "I like the way you play, young man. Do you have a telephone number?"

I said "Yes," and wrote down my phone number.

She said, "Someone's going to be in touch with you." A couple days later, her secretary called me to explain that Betty was going to be holding auditions for a new pianist, and that she wanted me to come out to Brooklyn so that she could hear me. I had a couple of weeks to prepare. I didn't have much money at all, but with what little cash I had, I went to the used-record store and spent it on Betty Carter records. I noticed that John Hicks was on quite a few of them. I got a great two-record set by Betty Carter called *The Audience* [Verve, 1980]. It was a live recording made in San Francisco with John Hicks and the drummer playing with me in my trio now, Kenny Washington. He was about nineteen on this record. (I didn't know we'd be playing together eventually.) I just really lived and slept with those records. I put them on cassette, and I would listen to them on my Walkman headphones at night when I was in bed. I would practice along. I noticed there was a real axis of communication going on between Betty Carter and John Hicks, musically. It was very apparent. I tried as best I could to sort of assimilate that feeling of what John Hicks was doing along with her.

The day of my audition arrived. I came in, and the drummer was the great Lewis Nash. He was twenty-five at the time, and I'd just turned twenty. I had never played with such a slick drummer before. It was such a wonderful feeling, just so buoyant and inspiring. Betty introduced us and said we should play something between ourselves. She said she was taking some food down to the kitchen, and she would be up in a while. But of course she was listening! But I was just so excited to be playing with Lewis that for a moment I forgot it was an audition. We just played. Then Betty came upstairs, after maybe twenty minutes or so, and she said, "You guys sound like you're having fun!" She said, "Let's try reading some things," and she pulled out a few charts. After maybe about the third tune, she said, "Okay, I'm satisfied. Would you like to join the band?" I was so excited! Practically speechless, I indicated "yes" by sort of nodding slowly. So the audition became my first rehearsal.

Betty was about to sing a ballad with us, a short time after that first audition, when she said, "Okay, gentlemen, when we play this next song, I want each of you to think about the last time you made love." Then she looked at me—I probably looked like a deer in the headlights—and she said, "You just use your imagination," which was what I did. Everyone else was thinking about the last time that they made love, and I was imagining what that would feel like; yet, when we played the song, somehow we were all on the same page.

Betty used to say, "Some of the things I ask you for, the male instrumentalists are not going to talk about." She was right! She was right on with that. A male instrumentalist wouldn't ever say, "Think about the last time you made love when you play this song." They'll just give you the changes and count it off. Betty would use these visuals with us, and that really formed the music. Because, of course, all music is an expression of life. If you channel any emotion honestly, people will feel it.

Case in point, as I am fond of citing: Just think about Ray Charles. None of us have lived his life, by any means. However, whether he's playing the piano, or singing, or both, somehow when we hear Ray Charles's music, we feel like we get it; we feel like we've been there. It's the pain and the sorrow and the joy and the victory. It's all the emotions. We feel like, we can totally relate to what he's talking about. How? We're not blind, we didn't grow up in the South, we're not him. I think that the bridge in music is honesty. If you're honestly channeling your life experiences, it doesn't matter what language people speak; it doesn't matter how much or how little they know about jazz—they will feel you. And that's what music is for.

I'm very thankful to these people who saw—if not a particular talent or a particular aptitude—how earnestly I wanted to be a part of this music. And I am so thankful that they chose to include me in the folds of what they do.

Is the life that you are living bigger than the one you had envisioned for yourself?

Absolutely. My goal was to be on that bandstand with Art Blakey. It didn't extend beyond that. I didn't know that from

Art Blakey I'd get to play with the greatest jazz trumpet player ever in his time, Freddie Hubbard, who had been a Jazz Messenger himself. I met Freddie through Art, and he invited me to join his band. I didn't know that I'd get to be a bandleader myself and, as a leader, a recording artist. And after playing with the hardest-swinging drummer in the history of jazz, Art Blakey, I certainly didn't know that I'd get to work for four-and-a-half years, my longest gig as a sideman ever, with the hardest-swinging bassist in the history of jazz, Mr. Ray Brown. I didn't see all that.

What have you learned about your character as a result of being in this business?

Well, it's ongoing. I'm learning all the time. The music does not come from us; it comes through us. One's ego can be a catalyst, or it can completely obstruct the spiritual flow of music. As musicians, as performers, we're constantly working to find a balance with our egos. You need an ego to manifest the attitude of walking on stage and, in effect, saying to the audience, "I have something worthy of your paying money for, and worthy of your time right now." It takes an ego to get up there and do that! At the same time, I could go on at great length with just a partial listing of all the great pianists who have inspired me, and continue to inspire me, that I don't hold a candle to. So there's that realizing the greatness of our musical heroes, and yet realizing gratitude and a sense of responsibility in the present moment, to deliver the music to people who want to feel something.

Also, I would say the number-one lesson that I've learned as a human, in life, is that I need to practice. I can't say that I'm as diligent these days as I used to be, and I would benefit by doing so, if I were. I was really a "practice fiend" back in the day, when I was with Betty. Betty loved it, and she used to say to me, "Practice as much as you can now. It's great that you like practicing because who knows what is going to be going on later on in your life? You could be married, with kids. You could have other responsibilities, business-wise." She said, "You're laying the foundation right now. The more practicing and studying you do now, the better off you'll be in the future." And those words were golden.

Look at athletes, people that really pushed themselves when they were teenagers, and how they maintain a certain kind of frame for their whole life, even if they don't work at it. You ride the momentum.

Was there anyone who said that you wouldn't be able to make it in the music business—what was your response to him or her?

Nope.

Were there times when you thought that you might not make it yourself?

There are moments, ongoing, when I'll listen to one of my heroes. I remember a few months ago, I was listening to Sonny Clark playing piano on a 1962 recording with the tenor saxophonist Ike Quebec, doing the ballad, "I've Got a Crush on You" [*Easy Living*, Blue Note Records, 1962]. What he played on a technical level was so simple, and yet there was so much feeling in it. I was just depressed for two days! I was like, "Wow, what am I even doing? That's real music; that's beautiful." What he was playing on this record was so profound and beautiful. Nothing complex, it was just real. It was serving notice to me—here and now, with all the innovations that have occurred since then, all the amazing things that have happened in music since 1962—just the stark honesty and simplicity that he was playing with.

What, for you, was the most unexpected aspect about being a professional musician?

The loneliness of being a musician. Because it's such an ethereal feeling to be onstage playing music and bringing happiness and connecting with the other musicians. Wonderful spontaneous things are happening, and the audience is appreciative. Then you go back to a hotel room by yourself. And repeating that. At first it was cool: "Awesome, I get to watch my own TV as much as I want late at night!"

Then it kind of got a lot deeper over the decades. Different musicians and traveling performers find ways of utilizing the time or coping with the loneliness or the isolation, be it drinking, or womanizing, or what have you. I'm not drawn to either one. I've really never been interested in casual dating; I've always been a relationship kind of person. Sustaining romantic relationships over a long distance has been a great challenge. I'm really thankful that I'm finding some balance with that. I feel very loved and very cared for by a few very special people in my life who really understand who I am, and my sensitivities, what it's like for me, what I'm dealing with. I feel very blessed and supported in my path.

If you were able, at this point in your life, to leave a note for your younger self when you were just starting out, what would the note say?

Listen more. And practice. I need to do much more of both. I take both for granted, and they are both the best medicines. Any serious, earnest, self-respecting jazz musician should listen to real jazz records every day and practice their instruments every day. And challenge themselves every day. If one is not doing that, one should really question if one really loves this music. If you love the music, you're going to want to listen to records because it feels so good. If that feels like an assignment, or drudgery, maybe you don't love it.

Do you have a favorite quote that inspires or motivates you?

I have two, and both of them come from the same former-girlfriend. One is in reference to our processes and growth. She used to say, "It's not a doing, it's an undoing." I think about that one a lot.

The other one that she said, which I found so beautiful, is, "Our life lessons keep coming around again and again, but they will come in a more painful form until we take heed." You're drawn to a certain kind of person and relationship, there's some kind of mystique or appeal, and yet it's not actually a spiritually conducive vibe for you. You might be burned a little bit. But if you don't realize what it was that's not copacetic for you, you might be attracted to those same qualities again.

What does music mean to you?

More than I know how to say. More than I have yet to realize. Music is a bridge between two people. When words fail us, there's music. I'm so grateful to have music in my life. Music inspires me to want to be a better person, to address my character, my ability to receive and give with people. It all comes through in the music.

Bob Mintzer

---◆---

Birthdate: January 27, 1953

Birthplace: New Rochelle, New York

Main instruments: Tenor saxophone, bass clarinet

Other instruments: Clarinet, drums, piano, flute, EWI

Website: www.bobmintzer.com

How long have you been a professional musician?

My first professional gig was in 1970, with the Concord Hotel Catskill Mountains dance band. My first professional gig of notoriety was with Eumir Deodato in 1974.

Have you had to support yourself with other jobs, or has music been your only profession?

I drove a taxi while in music school. But after leaving school, I made my living solely by playing music. I did any and every gig I could to pay my bills. This went on for quite a while. Between the good gigs, I did some questionable ones, like we all do at one time or another. It wasn't until I was forty years old that I started to play creative music all the time.

What drew you to playing the saxophone?

Hearing the great jazz saxophonists play around New York City was the initial inspiration. I got to hear Sonny Rollins, Dexter Gordon, Sonny Stitt, Rahsaan Roland Kirk, George Coleman, etc. Hearing John Coltrane, Lester Young, and Ben Webster on recordings provided further inspiration and pointed me in the direction of the tenor saxophone.

I played other instruments before saxophone. I actually started on clarinet, and I played piano and guitar as well. Initially I played primarily classical music and some Dixieland jazz on the clarinet. I later played rock and roll and blues on the guitar before delving into the world of jazz.

Ultimately what attracted me to saxophone was becoming more familiar with jazz music and recognizing the role of the tenor saxophone in the music. I just felt that my voice would come out on that instrument. I was hearing things in terms of playing the tenor saxophone versus the other instruments that I had played.

What drew you to jazz music?

I liked the fact that jazz appeared to contain elements of all kinds of music. I was attracted to rhythm and blues, Tin Pan Alley, and classical music. Jazz seemed to be some sort of mix of all these different styles that I had already had some exposure to. It was all done in a very spontaneous way where there was an "in the moment" interaction amongst the players. There was a certain level of intensity and excitement that really attracted me.

BOB'S MUSICAL NOTES

♪ Bob received the Grammy award for best large jazz ensemble recording in 2001, for *Homage to Count Basie* (DMP Records, 2000). He has had four other Grammy nominations.

♪ He has written more than two hundred big band arrangements.

♪ Bob currently resides in Los Angeles in the former home of composer Arnold Schoenberg.

♪ He enjoys hiking, cooking and eating with friends, reading, and skiing.

Jazz music typically requires a very high level of musicianship and virtuosity on one's instrument—the ability to really comprehend the big picture (composition, form, orchestration). I guess every kind of music requires a high level of proficiency and artistry, but jazz music in particular, where you are improvising and interacting in the moment, demands a fluidity that comes only with years of study and playing the music with others. This presented a great challenge that I was drawn to.

Who played the most significant role in your musical development? Why?

I heard John Coltrane (on recording) play and that was a big attraction to playing the saxophone. I heard Sonny Rollins play several times live around New York. I heard Wayne Shorter play with the Miles Davis Quintet, when I was fourteen, and that really made a big impression. I heard Dexter Gordon and Rahsaan Roland Kirk play around New York when I was in my teens. All of those great saxophonists were very attractive to me and made me want to pursue playing music.

I met Roland Kirk several times. I sat in with him when I was very young and got my ass kicked. Rahsaan was very generous towards young musicians. He did me a huge favor letting me sit in. I've had conversations with Sonny Rollins and Ornette Coleman, both dedicated and inspired individuals, to say the least! I knew Jackie McLean pretty well; he taught at Hart College when I was a student there. He was really very supportive and inspirational. I knew and got to work a bit with Junior Cook, who was a great saxophonist. I know James Moody and Jimmy Heath, both wonderful saxophonists. I think all of the people that I've mentioned have been, and always were, dedicated students of art and music. And very humble people.

Just to illustrate, I would say fifteen years ago I went to hear James Moody play at a club in New York. At that time, he must have been in his late sixties. He finished the set and came over to say hello. He then asked me, "How did I sound?" I was taken aback. Here was a veteran of jazz approaching me with the question of how he sounded, when clearly I was the student, and he the teacher. I remember thinking, why are you asking me this? But I was honored and flattered that he was. By the way, I responded to him, "You sound great!" It was very touching and a wonderful example of humility and a lifelong quest to be a better musician. I'll never forget that lesson.

As a teacher, I feel like I learn a lot from my students, as well. I like to keep a dialogue going where I am attuned to what their needs are and how we might improve upon the teacher/student situation. So I am constantly asking for feedback and asking what the students would like to do differently. I think the main role of a teacher is to inspire and to get students excited to the point where they want to put in the time and the work to do their own research. This was the gift my teachers presented to me.

Is the life that you are living bigger than the one you had envisioned for yourself?

The only vision that I had when I was younger was to be an accomplished musician and, hopefully, get to play a lot. I wasn't sure if this was a realistic expectation or not. Thankfully, I was obsessed enough with music to have the drive to spend most of each day practicing and learning as much as I could. If an opportunity came along to play in a band, I jumped at the chance, and gratefully so. Playing in one band frequently leads to playing in other bands, and this was the case for me. Through these encounters, I was able to move from [Eumir] Deodato to Tito Puente, to Buddy Rich, to the Thad Jones/Mel Lewis Big Band, to Jaco Pastorius, to the Yellowjackets, and on from there.

I had the opportunity to start my own big band some twenty-eight years ago. It wasn't even really something I had intended to do. As a saxophonist, I was more focused on trying to play in a quartet or a quintet setting, where a saxophonist gets far more solo space. I had been in big bands earlier in my career with Buddy Rich and Thad and Mel.

In 1983, an opportunity came along to put a big band together to play in New York. On a lark I called all my favorite musicians: Dave Sanborn, Mike and Randy Brecker, Peter Erskine, Will Lee, Don Grolnick, Lew Soloff. The band became an immediate success. So I just thought, well, I'll do this for now. It's here, and it's up and running. I followed the opportunity, and as a result, have had a big band for all these years. It's created a sizeable level of activity, including writing, playing, guest conducting, and having my music performed all over the world. I had no idea this would happen!

What have you learned about your character as a result of being in this business?

I'm a hard worker. I have something to offer. I'm a decent human being. People seem to like to work with me. I learned to be grateful for every day I get to play music. I've learned that it is okay to not know all there is to know, and to not be afraid to ask for help. These are the traits that I observed in the musicians I had the great fortune to work with.

Was there anyone who said that you wouldn't be able to make it in the music business—what was your response to him or her?

A few. Just a few. Really, the only one that comes to mind is somebody that kind of looked at me as a competitor. It wasn't even in jazz; it was in the studio scene in New York. But, by and large, most of the people that I encountered were very supportive and encouraging. I'm really grateful for that.

I certainly try to be that way. I see no reason for trying to discourage somebody from following their passion, even if it is clear to me that their level is not what it perhaps should be. If I sense that somebody is really engaged and enthralled with what they are doing, I see no reason to discourage that person.

I was on the faculty of Rutgers University for a year back in the eighties, and they had a policy that if a student was really not doing the work, you would issue a warning. If, after two weeks, there was no change, you would recommend that they be removed from the program. I had such a student. I gave him the warning, and after no such discernible change, I recommended that he be removed from the program. And he was.

So, fast-forward about fifteen years, and I'm playing a concert with the Yellowjackets in Philadelphia. There is an opening band, and I hear somebody warming up on the saxophone. I go over to see who it is and introduce myself. I say, "Hey, how are you doing? I'm Bob Mintzer. And who are you?"

He said, "You should know who I am. You threw me out of college!" This guy really snapped into gear after that incident and said, "I'm going to show everybody that I can do this!" He became quite an accomplished saxophonist and musician. He was the exception to the rule, but I'm glad that it happened that way. It was great to see him doing well.

Were there times when you thought that you might not make it yourself?

There still are. I'm fairly accepting of my musicianship, but I think that right before a growth spurt I become, as do many musicians, dissatisfied with whatever it is I'm doing and feel like I need to rejuvenate my vocabulary and to look for other things and other approaches to playing and writing and thinking about music.

It generally has a good effect. I acknowledge that I've been doing this a long time, and I've reached a certain level, but it by no means feels like anything final. It's kind of a step along the way. There's still a long way to go.

I never quite looked at it like, "I've made it." I looked at it more like, "I'm okay today, and I've got to work at it really hard to get better and to keep this thing moving forward."

What, for you, was the most unexpected aspect about being a professional musician?

I think as musicians we are very self-critical and always hyper-vigilant about what we are doing and how we sound, and how we can improve upon it. I know, personally, I'm kind of surprised when people like what I'm doing, musically. That's always sort of unexpected because I am always looking at it with a critical eye, thinking, I could have done this better. It's always an unexpected and pleasant surprise when somebody appreciates something you've done.

Also, what's unexpected, at least from the early stages, was that traveling and playing would be such a great thing, where you get to learn about other cultures and meet people from all over the world. That's really a fantastic part of being a musician. The traveling is hard, but being in new places and meeting people and experiencing things is wonderful.

If you were able, at this point in your life, to leave a note for your younger self when you were just starting out, what would the note say?

I guess the note would say: Everything is going to be okay.

Just keep moving forward. And try to enjoy life the best you can.

Do you have a favorite quote that inspires or motivates you?

I have a couple, actually. One is: "To try and live in the moment." Another one is: "Something is what it is." Occasionally, in the name of some sort of educational endeavor, I work with a band of less than stellar musicians, and I have a choice at that point. I can focus on how not great they sound, or on how much better they sound now than they did before the first rehearsal. I just try to see the positive aspect of a situation. I look at it like, well, they invited me to come work with them, and I'm being compensated in a beautiful place, and we are all doing the best we can. And that's enough.

What does music mean to you?

It's a form of expression. It's a form of spirituality. It's a means of making contact with other people, sometimes people who don't even speak the same spoken language as you. It's a means of reaching people in a profound way that perhaps evokes some sort of thought process or emotional sensation. It's a way to instill a positive message in young people who appreciate your music—a way to kind of slip in a little message, along the lines of, "Do the right thing and try to do the best you can."

Kendrick Scott

◆

Birthdate: July 8, 1980

Birthplace: Houston

Main instrument: Drums

Website: www.kendrickscott.com

How long have you been a professional musician?

I would say since 2003. I went straight from Berklee College of Music and started playing. I've been playing since I was a kid and played in church. I don't know if that would be considered professional, but in a way, it is.

Have you had to support yourself with other jobs, or has music been your only profession?

Music has been my only profession.

What drew you to the drums?

I always tell people I didn't choose them; they chose me. I

KENDRICK'S MUSICAL NOTES

♪ In 2007, Kendrick launched his own record label, World Culture Music, with the release of his first album, *The Source*. Kendrick made the album as leader of his own band, Kendrick Scott Oracle.

♪ He was winner of a Clifford Brown/Stan Getz Fellow in 1999, an award whose purpose is to foster young musical talent and to promote jazz as an art form.

♪ Wayne Shorter is his biggest idol.

♪ Basketball is a major hobby of Kendrick's. He says "its relation to teamwork, in music and in life, always connects with me."

think it was a certain calling. My mother and my brother played the piano; my father played the trombone.

At church, I was always just called to the drums. When church was over, I would immediately just go to the drum set and stand there and look at it. The guy who played at our church had the coolest drum set. They were big, loud drums. They just looked cool.

I definitely think it was my calling. It was nothing that happened by accident. I never experienced anything like that in my life, other than being called to play the drums.

What drew you to jazz music?

At age fourteen, I was at a crossroads. My plan was to go to a certain high school called Willowridge. In Texas and Louisiana, marching bands are huge. Willowridge had one of the best marching bands in Houston, and the football team was great. The band would travel to the Rose Bowl, and they would play at all of these great marching festivals. I wanted to go on to Southern University and A&M College or Prairie View A&M— all these historically black colleges with great bands. Then my mom kind of broke it down and said, "How many professional marching band drummers do you see?" It was one of those things where Mom had to come in and lay down the law. She said, "That's not a profession, it's a hobby."

So at fourteen, I tried out for the High School for the Performing and Visual Arts, and I made it in. I learned how to play "Seven Steps to Heaven" [Miles Davis, *Seven Steps to Heaven*, Columbia Records, 1963], and I tuned my drums to the pitches. My teachers helped me, and I got in. That's when jazz became paramount. Before then, it was mostly gospel music. I'd heard some jazz, but it really wasn't a big thing for me.

When I went to school, I would say jazz was another calling. It just hit me. There wasn't a certain point, or anything, where I thought, "I want to play jazz." It was just like, "Wow, this is it!" That's when I knew I would play the drums forever. I knew that was going to be my profession when I entered high school. It was good knowing that, but it was a scary thing, too, because you feel like your options are limited in some ways. I only wanted to do this one thing. But what else did I love?

I'm a person; I don't want to be defined as a musician only. But in essence, that's the way I communicate with the world. I constantly am still struggling with it today. Among all other ways of communication, music is still the way I communicate. In that sense, I'm very happy about it. And being a jazz musician is cool, too!

Who played the most significant role in your musical development? Why?

I would have to say Terence Blanchard. Before I got into jazz, I was in the marching band, and there were two guys who helped me out, before Terence. One was my middle school teacher, Jimmie Jacobs. In middle school, my mom and Mr. Jacobs had a pact: if I ever got out of line, my ass was his. So he used to paddle me, but it actually turned out to be pretty cool.

The story of how I got to the school was that my parents divorced when I was eleven. I was leaving elementary school, so my first year of middle school was at—I don't want to say an "uppity" school, but it was just so different. It was really different. Then the next year, I got transferred to, for lack of a word, a "ghetto" school. So my last year of middles school was at this "ghetto" school.

It was a complete "*Lean on Me*" moment, because Mr. Jacobs was the best thing for me, at that time. He just kind of kept me in line when I wanted to run with a wild crowd. I've always been enthralled with being in the wrong crowd, especially at that school because it was cool to be in the wrong crowd. So Mr. Jacobs kept me on the straight and narrow. He was almost sacrificing his job to whoop my ass into shape. For all of his students, he would take that time and talk with us. If anything went wrong in somebody else's class, the teachers wouldn't send us to the principal; they would send us to the band room. The consequences were greater to go to Mr. Jacobs than to go to the principal.

He was really, really important for my musical world, also. He definitely helped that. Mr. Jacobs was into a lot of gospel music and a little bit of jazz. I would think, musically, he is one of my people. Music always meant something more to him.

Then, before Mr. Jacobs, there was my mother. As far as my practicing and being serious about music, she was the *main* influence. I felt I could make a living out of it when I was a young kid, and I've got to give it all to my mom. My mom was probably the number one influence from the beginning, then Mr. Jacobs.

At the same time, I started taking lessons from a guy named Darryl Singleton, who is a percussion teacher at Texas Southern University. That also added to my wanting to be in the marching band because he was into all that stuff. He was very pivotal in exposing me to jazz more than I had been. He went to Howard University in D.C., and he exposed me to some things that were really great; plus he got my technique together.

Then when I entered high school, Bob Morgan became my mentor. So many great jazz musicians went there: Robert Glasper, Beyoncé, Jason Moran, Eric Harland, Chris Dave, Bryan-Michael Cox. So many amazing musicians were there, so it was great to be there. Just having the experience of being around other people who are doing what you are doing, and doing it well, creates a healthy competition, too

But Terence has been my greatest musical influence. He took my talent to where it is by cultivating my creativity and not just my knowledge. I was a very studied student; but in some aspects, if you're not bringing yourself to it, if you're not bringing your heart to it, music makes no sense.

But there are times when people can get away with that, for a whole career, even. Because people can pick up an instrument, and they can learn how to play it, and they can play the hell out of it for the rest of their lives, and never really say what they have to say. Terence helped me with that.

Every big thing that I've done has been through Terence. I went on tour with Herbie [Hancock] for three months, and I got that gig through Terence. I played with Dianne Reeves, and that was through Terence. All of my connections have come through Terence, all of my film scores. It's just been great. He encouraged me to do my first CD. Everything, really.

Is the life that you are living bigger than the one you had envisioned for yourself?

It's actually *smaller*, but it's just as great. When I was a kid, I was enthralled with child prodigies. I always wanted to be a prodigy, to be that little kid who was great at what he does. When I was sixteen, I met this guy, Thomas Pridgen, from California. I think he was three or four years younger than I was. I've never been *that much* into my ability; I'm still not. I think I am an "okay" drummer.

This fool came in and played the craziest drum set that I've ever seen. He murdered the drums. I was like, "What is going on?" He was probably thirteen or fourteen! When I saw that, I wanted to be *that* guy—the one that just murders the drums. My aspirations were like that: "I am going to be the best drummer *ever*." So by the time I was twenty, I wanted to be in Stevie Wonder's band; I wanted to do this, I wanted to do that.

But I've been blessed for things to have happened in the way that they did. I could never have imagined things happening this way. But still, when I was a kid, I was thinking of things on some grander scale. Again, it's realizing what my calling is. After a while, I realized, "You weren't called to be that guy, to be that drummer. As much as you practice, as much as you learn, you could never be that guy." Then it hit me: "That's right, I could never be that guy, and I don't want to be that guy." But whenever I go to hear him, it just reminds me how much I wanted to be like him. And not just him, specifically, but to be part of the whole mystique of it. To be a kid and be the greatest in world—I wanted to be that kid!

What have you learned about your character as a result of being in this business?

I've learned that I am pretty honest, even to a fault. I'm honest in a business sense and honest with my music. I think my music reflects who I am as a person. I think I've been more and more able to relate to people and everything through my music, so it also opens me up personally to people.

Being honest and true to myself is paramount at this moment. So when I think of anybody who is inspiring to me as a great musician, that is one character trait that I think they should have. I really have worked on that, for myself—the honesty thing.

Was there anyone who said that you wouldn't be able to make it in the music business—what was your response to him or her?

No, not really. Well, there is someone that I hold a grudge towards, to this day. There was a guy who came and did a clinic at my high school. Essentially, he was like, "What the hell are you playing?" That was a pivotal moment in my life.

First of all, I'm not a cocky person, but I am confident. I think that this guy probably messed up a lot of people. At the time, I was trying to find my voice and was experimenting with my music. As a kid, you want to experiment. This guy was totally like, "What are you doing? None of that makes any sense. That totally sucks." Essentially, he was saying: You're not learning the jazz that I know, that I know how to play. So it sucks because I don't know what it is.

That kind of discouraged me in high school. That's why I learned so much vocabulary, because I was like, "Okay, forget you. If you want me to play like Philly Joe Jones, I'm going to learn it." That mentality carried throughout high school.

When I joined Terence's band after college, none of that made any sense. It took me almost a year to open up. Terence was telling me, "You don't have to play like anybody else. You can just go ahead and do what you feel." And that is so different from how jazz is taught in school where we romanticize so many people. If you don't play like Art Blakey, you don't know how to play the drums. You know what I mean? Those are our idols, but at some point we have to get away from them. It's hard treading that thin line, but luckily I made it through that.

Were there times when you thought that you might not make it yourself?

Never.

What, for you, was the most unexpected aspect about being a professional musician?

I can't really think of anything. I was brought up in a household of musicians, so I kind of saw how things were happening. I grew up watching my mom play gigs, play in church, move around, and be a Renaissance woman.

If you were able, at this point in your life, to leave a note for your younger self when you were just starting out, what would the note say?

It would say: Be yourself. Keep practicing and be yourself. And cherish people. Relationships are one of those things that I'm still working on, as a person, with my parents, friends, everybody. I think that relates to my music, too. A musical mind is a lonely mind. It can go off into its own space at any point. I think that cherishing people, the people you are with, is as important as cherishing your musical mind. Developing those skills earlier, I think, would have been better for me.

Do you have a favorite quote that inspires or motivates you?

I have one that I put on my drumsticks. It's the beginning of a prayer. It says: "Lord, make me an instrument of Thy peace." It goes on, and there's a whole prayer behind it that I say when I play. I write it on all of my sticks, and it helps me put everything into perspective. When those thoughts come into my mind about being "that guy" again, when thoughts come in my mind about what gig am I playing, where am I playing, who am I playing with, or who am I trying to impress, that sentence puts everything into perspective for me. So I love to write that down where I can see it. When I'm warming up, I'll say the prayer. Every time I pick up a stick, I see it. It's on every stick; it's on every mallet. As soon as you get out of line—"Oh, I'm hot, I'm going to do this, and I'm going to do that"—then it's like, remember: *You* are the instrument, not the drums.

What does music mean to you?

I was blessed to be raised in a family where music was so important. The more and more I travel around the world, I realize that music is one of the fabrics of every culture. I feel that, even more than something like religion, music is paramount. It has that sort of effect, a spiritual effect, on people around the world. With all the divides that are in religion, when I look at music, there are none. As far as the acceptance, if I go to India, if I go to South Africa, if I go anywhere, my music is going to permeate all those divides. That's why I think music is the number one spiritual experience in life.

Again, I'm defining myself as a musician, which I am trying to get away from. I heard that Wayne Shorter said, "Music doesn't define me." And I'm trying to get there. He said, "Music is just one small portion of my life. I'm a being so much bigger than music."

I feel that way, and yet, music is so spiritual for me. If I didn't have that, it would be difficult to maintain that same spiritual position in life.

Mark Whitfield

✦

Birthdate: October 6, 1966

Birthplace: Lindenhurst, New York

Main instrument: Guitar

Other instruments: Bass, saxophone

Website: www.markwhitfield.com

How long have you been a professional musician?

Since 1985 at a private party in Seattle with Woody Woodhouse, at age fifteen.

Have you had to support yourself with other jobs, or has music been your only profession?

I did have a regular job. I worked as a prospector for a stockbroker at Bear Stearns on Wall Street. My sister was a stockbroker; she got me the job. You have to pay the bills somehow.

MARK'S MUSICAL NOTES

♪ Mark is featured along with R&B guitarist Joel Kipnis, who is commonly known in the industry as JK, on the DVD, *The Jazz Channel Presents Soul Conversation Featuring Mark Whitfield & JK.*

♪ Mark was given the nickname "Quik Pick" by his friend, bass player David Dyson, because of his extraordinary speed while playing the guitar.

♪ On stage, Mark plays a bright, cherry-red guitar, custom designed for him by Stephen Marchione.

♪ Mark's musical family includes his sons, drummer Mark Jr., who begins graduate studies at the Manhattan School of Music on a full scholarship in fall 2011; and pianist Davis, who was awarded a Presidential scholarship to attend the Berklee College of Music beginning fall 2011.

What drew you to the guitar?

The instrument itself was a gift. When I was seven, my brother, Davis, gave it to me after he himself had received the guitar as a homecoming present when his tour in Vietnam was done. I didn't think I had any interest in playing an instrument. But this was my brother, and he handed me the guitar and said, "Here's the blues." Then he handed me a copy of a Lightnin' Hopkins blues record, *Anthology of the Blues: Lightnin' Hopkins, A Legend In His Own Time* [Kent Records, 1969] and said, "Here's how it is supposed to go. Give it a shot."

If my big brother said try it, I tried it. I had a real connection to the instrument, but I was just interested in playing it as a hobby. But one thing is for sure; I definitely had a real interest in the guitar and in any understanding of music.

I also checked out the alto saxophone in fourth-grade marching band and concert band ensemble. In fifth grade, I started playing the bass. So I played all three instruments at the same time. Once you have an understanding of how music works, it can be relatively easy to transfer that from instrument to instrument. But it helps that the bass and the guitar are closely related. They have nothing to do with the saxophone, though. I got pretty good at the saxophone and improved quickly. I played it for a couple of years but gave it up when the guitar became much more important to me.

I still feel like playing the guitar is an ongoing challenge. Every time I play it, I feel like there is something I still need to address. There are still things I need to improve, things that I need to explore. That's the part that makes it the most fun.

What drew you to jazz music?

My parents were fans of jazz since I was a little kid. I can remember hearing my parents' records since I was four or five.

I grew up on Long Island, and they took me to the Westbury Music Center. It was a concert hall, basically, and it had a revolving stage. I saw groups like Duke Ellington and the Count Basie Band. I saw Oscar Peterson there. Watching these great musicians, in the moment, gave me an ear for the sound and an appreciation of the musicians for how difficult it had to be to play an instrument, or to sing or perform well, at that level.

There are things about playing jazz music that are unique. Being able to respond to what is being played around you is something that I find unique to playing jazz.

Classical musicians play their part. In a lot of ways, in pop music, you play your part. You can go louder or go faster, depending on what's happening around you. But your ability to respond and react within the framework of the music that you are playing is limited based on the genre. One of the things about jazz is that it takes that limitation away and provides all sorts of possibilities. So I bring that to whoever I am playing with, whether it is Chris Botti, or Sting, or Steven Tyler, or Yo-Yo Ma. I bring the idea that there are more than just the obvious possibilities.

Who played the most significant role in your musical development? Why?

First it was my music teachers: Ray Williams, Dominic Attisani and Julie Ruben. Ray Williams was the orchestra and jazz band director at my elementary school, and he introduced me to Julie Ruben. Julie was the junior high school band and all-star director. Dominic Attisani taught at the high school, and he was the marching band director. He was the music director for the town.

Looking back, now that I also teach as well, I realize how well they provided a really strong foundation in music for me. I look back at some of the groups that I was involved in and the things that we were able to accomplish at fourteen, fifteen, sixteen years old. I realize that they were very instrumental in laying the groundwork for me to have an understanding of how easy it could be to make good music if you paid attention to detail. I had great teachers in the beginning, and they provided me with the skills that would then make becoming a professional musician possible.

From there on, my influences moved from music teachers to people who taught me more about music. I had a history teacher my last year of high school named Harry Atkins who introduced me to the sound of Charlie Christian's guitar. Charlie was a member of Benny Goodman's group. That got me going. Taking what I heard from Charlie Christian and what I saw from people on television, I then moved on to the sound of Joe Pass, and then eventually to one and all of the masters in jazz music, everyone from Duke Ellington to John Coltrane to Miles Davis. Once you start what I consider to be an organized study of jazz, it happens chronologically by decade. I studied it that way, and each decade, each period, became influential.

Finally, I got to a point where I was influenced by musicians who were still living, and who became most important to me on the guitar. The former *The Tonight Show* bandleader Kevin Eubanks is one of the true living legends on guitar. I met him my first year of college. He had gone to Berklee a few years before I did, and he came back to teach a master class. I asked a few questions, and I was having some difficulty with my right arm. He helped solve the problem, and he offered to give me a private lesson. He just took me under his wing, and he was very, very inspirational for a kid at sixteen, seventeen, eighteen, who was struggling to put the pieces together.

It's funny about jazz, which I think makes it different from every other style of music. We can teach you how to play jazz. We can help you assemble the various building blocks, but you have to figure out how to put them together yourself. There is no shortcut. There is no cheating your way through. So every step of the way, I had someone whose influence was profound enough that they helped me understand the next level of puzzle-solving, because that's what jazz is. It is a really long puzzle that you find new ways to solve. So Kevin helped me quite a bit with that.

Shortly after graduating, I met George Benson, who, of course, was my hero. There were no other musicians in my family, so I never considered becoming a professional musician until my teenage years, when I realized it was something that I should do for a living. Then I saw George Benson performing on television, in a **PBS** special with the Boston Pops, in, I want to say, 1977 or 1978. And that really set me on fire. I was playing guitar, but I was also playing bass and saxophone. At that point, I dropped everything and turned my attention solely to guitar. I set my sights on emulating George Benson. He became my hero at that point.

George really helped over the next few years from when I was nineteen or twenty to around age twenty-four, twenty-five. He really helped me put the finishing touches on the puzzle and helped me to identify and establish my sound as a musician. He helped set me on the course that has carried me this far.

I got to meet him when I was about twenty. It was very unexpected. One of my first gigs was in New York because I had moved here after college; I worked at the jazz club Blue Note at night. That was when they had late night sets. The regular show went from eight or nine until about eleven o'clock or midnight, and the late-night band would come on around twelve-thirty or one; we would play until about four in the morning. We played Tuesday through Sunday night, and we did that for about fifteen or twenty bucks apiece, but it was more about the idea that we were playing in a great location.

I got to meet so many great musicians—that was what made it special. One night, I guess within the first two months of when I started working there, they were having the annual anniversary celebration. Billy Eckstine and his band were playing for the week, and he had some special guests on the actual night of the anniversary. He had Tony Bennett; Chaka Khan was there, and George Benson was coming.

So it was our job as the late-night band during this particular event to entertain the crowd during the break. They went on and played an hour, we came on and played half an hour, that kind of thing. George did show up, and he came without a guitar. The club owner said to me, "Hey man, George Benson is here, and he wants to play. Do you mind if we let him use your guitar?" Believe me, I did not mind! I had only one condition—that I got to meet him.

One of George's sons had gone to Berklee, and I knew him in passing, so we talked a bit about that. George played, and he was great, of course. When he got finished, he handed me back my guitar and said, "Well, I'd love to stick around and hear you, but my wife and I have someplace else to go. I am sure I will see you around."

I was relieved—I was scared because it was George Benson—but I was also very disappointed that I didn't get a chance to play for my hero. Turns out, he was just saying that so I wouldn't be nervous. He had gone and stood by the door, and he watched me play.

After the show ended, he left me a note saying he liked what he heard, and that I would see him again. A couple of weeks later, he came back and gave me his phone number. I started to call him and talk to him. He picked me up in his Rolls one day, and we went to his house. He started unofficially giving me a guitar lesson. He helped me to get a lot of things together in a very short period of time. And when he thought I was ready, he introduced me to Tommy LiPuma at Warner Brothers. He facilitated my very first record deal. [*Marksman*, Warner Brothers/WEA, 1990]. It was a wonderful time.

We became very good friends. I make sure I speak to him

every month. I've told him I appreciate him so often that he's tired of hearing it. He says, "Yeah, yeah, yeah, I get it."

Is the life that you are living bigger than the one you had envisioned for yourself?

It's different. I never really had a blueprint for success. I just had a vision of what it would be like to do nothing but play music for a living. I was drawn to jazz and classical music. I thought if I could just perform music, I'd be all right. I never really thought I'd have the chance to make a lot of money, or to meet a lot of celebrities, or even travel the world. I was just hoping I'd be able to move to New York after going to college, and I was hoping to go explore my options and play guitar. The ultimate journey that I've embarked on has been quite a surprise. And a huge bonus.

My hopes had started out very simply. Even once I realized there was an opportunity for me to become a professional musician and actually make a living doing what I love to do, I still envisioned much more humble surroundings for myself.

What have you learned about your character as a result of being in this business?

In a sink-or-swim situation, I have the capacity to keep on swimming—and to carry folks with me. I had always wondered how I would fare in a tight spot, where things are on the line. I am happy to say that at every crossroads, when the left was sink and the right was swim, I swam and I pulled through. Sometimes that meant carrying my family, or carrying a loved one, or just supporting a friend. It's not always just about standing up on your own two feet. Sometimes you have the weight of the world on your shoulders, and you can't let people down. I'm happy to say that I've managed to persevere.

Being a parent, that has been really important to me to instill in my children. It has to come from within. But my parents—after watching them provide for me and struggling through the various stages in my own life—I realized they inspired me to be stronger, to have heart, and to be steady and consistent—to be the kind of person my sons could look up to.

Was there anyone who said that you wouldn't be able to make it in the music business—what was your response to him or her?

No. My parents were concerned that I might not be able to survive the pitfalls of a life in the music industry, but I don't think they were ever concerned that I wouldn't be able to make it as a musician. Over the years, my parents befriended many musicians. My father was very close with a guy named Buck Clayton who played trumpet for Count Basie and for his own band.

My father, as a teenager, had aspirations of becoming a jazz singer. He did a lot of things back in the thirties and forties that were associated with music. My parents helped me to develop the strength of my character, to be able to wade through all the nonsense and still stick to the straight and narrow path, to be responsible enough to handle life as a musician.

Were there times when you thought that you might not make it yourself?

No, I never really lost hope. There were times when my career was a casualty of the turmoil in the industry. There were certain things that happened that presented unexpected challenges in terms of survival. But I've always subscribed to the theory that if I take care of the music, the music will take care of me. Things have worked out so far.

What, for you, was the most unexpected aspect about being a professional musician?

I don't think I was truly prepared for the challenge of making a living. I thank God that I started out so young that I was nearly oblivious to the actual struggles of it. It was something that I could not have done, if let's say, I had gone to college when I was twenty and I had started then. I couldn't have done it. There were just so many aspects to the struggle as a young musician, that I just would not have been willing to do it.

If you were able, at this point in your life, to leave a note for your younger self when you were just starting out, what would the note say?

To work hard with reckless abandon. There were moments when, even for the shortest time, I got sidetracked from my short-term goals. It may have been a concern about the industry, or family concerns, or something about my personal life that seemed to be way more important to me at the time than it wound up being in the grand scheme of things. So life presents you with a series of little mini-challenges, if you are fortunate enough to keep living. Getting older, I've realized that there were things that I considered to be so important and of such significance, that they took me away from things that I really should have been concerned with. The things ended up not really being very important at all. I would have been better served by not having my attention distracted.

It really helps being able to trudge forward with life sometimes. That's something I really admire about Chris [Botti]. He just trudges through with life, no matter what. His goals are unwavering, and his drive to accomplish those goals is unfaltering. He's a good person for me to work with, especially because a lot of goals that we have as individuals are in agreement. It works well.

Do you have a favorite quote that inspires or motivates you?

I remember a quote from Jack McDuff, who was a great jazz organist and the guy who gave George Benson his start. He was the first person that I really worked with at a professional event. From the time I was twenty-one to twenty-three, I was on the road with Jack, and it was a real launching pad for my career. One of the things that he taught me that will stick with me forever was that, "You only get out of music what you are willing to put in." He said you can't cheat.

I have known a lot of musicians along the way who have achieved a high level of commercial success with what seemed like very little blood, sweat and tears. It is also how you perceive the definition of success. As you get older, you realize that it's not always what it seems. I think it is universal in that no matter how successful a person is, or how much like an overnight success it may seem, no one ever gets more than what they put in. And I think that's a very, very good lesson to learn for young musicians, especially if you get discouraged when you see yourself working really hard, and you don't see the immediate return of your hard work. You look around, and you see what appears to be other people getting so much more out of so much less. Don't be fooled.

What does music mean to you?

Music is life. Music is inspiring; it is a place of refuge. It's a way that all people can connect. It breaks down the barriers of language and culture. I was amazed as a young musician when I first began to travel, how easy it was, how universally the music was accepted. How it transcends so many barriers. Music is part of the thread that makes who we are.

Craig Klein

✦

Birthdate: November 21, 1960

Birthplace: New Orleans

Main instrument: Trombone

Other instrument: Tuba

Website: www.boneramamusic.com

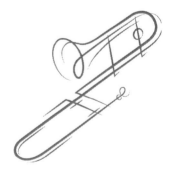

How long have you been a professional musician?

I started playing professionally with a funky, rocking, horn cover band in 1979.

Have you had to support yourself with other jobs, or has music been your only profession?

I graduated from college in 1984. I was playing music at that time, but I was also a real estate agent. I was selling real estate because I needed something; music wasn't just quite enough to make ends meet. I wasn't at that level, yet. I was getting some gigs, but it wasn't enough to support myself, and I had just got married.

In 1990, we had heard Harry Connick, Jr. was going to put together a band. Word gets around. Shannon Powell was a drummer, and he was in Harry's trio. Shannon was one of

CRAIG'S MUSICAL NOTES

♪ Craig, along with the other Bonerama Horns (Mark Mullins and Greg Hicks), appears on "It Happened Today" and "Oh My Heart" on R.E.M.'s *Collapse into Now* (Warner Brothers, 2011).

♪ In 2008, Bonerama released a joint EP with OK Go, titled *You're Not Alone* (Capitol, 2008), to raise money for New Orleans musicians still displaced by Hurricane Katrina.

♪ Craig practices yoga.

♪ When not busy playing music, he enjoys hanging out with his four children.

Harry's childhood friends, and he was telling me that Harry was putting together a big band because he had just recorded his record *We Are in Love* [Sony, 1990].

When Harry Met Sally [Sony, 1989] was his first big band record, so then he became more of a national name. That was done with studio musicians. Then he recorded *We Are in Love*, which had a lot of his own songs. He recorded that with studio musicians, too, but he was going to put a band together for six months to tour to support this record. So he wanted some New Orleans musicians—it's obvious why—as much as he loves New Orleans.

So he had Shannon, and then he hired Leroy [Jones] and Lucien Barbarin. He wanted some more musicians. Lucien didn't really read music, so Harry wanted other guys who did. Lucien and I were really close at that time, best friends. Lucien told me, "I'm going to try and get you in; I'm going to try and get you in the band."

I said, "Great, that's good!"

One day, Lucien told me to go home, that they were going to call me. So I was home and waiting for the phone to ring, and it was Ben Wolfe, who was Harry's bass player and the musical director at that time. Ben said, "We are putting a band together, and we want to hear you play. You can either send us a tape, or you can play over the phone right now."

I figured, it's either now or never. I told him, "I'll play for you right now." So I put the phone down and I played the song, I think it was a New Orleans song, called "Dr. Jazz."

So that was pretty much it. Ben told me, "You know, Harry was in the studio when I called, and we both listened. And Harry said, 'Hire him.'" So that's how I got it.

You have to sometimes be in the right place at the right time, and sometimes luck kind of falls your way. But you have to be prepared for it. It was just lucky how it happened, but I was ready for it at that time. Even though the tour was off and on, that six-month tour lasted sixteen years!

Harry takes off a lot of the time, but in New Orleans there were always projects with other musicians. One of the other trombone players, Mark Mullins, also auditioned over the phone for Harry. I had an idea, and I told Mark that I wanted to put a band together that features trombones, a trombone-fronted band.

When we were in New York with Harry, there was a club called the Village Gate, and every Monday night was "Salsa Meets Jazz." We spent a lot of time in New York because a lot of the stuff that we did just happened there. Whenever we were in New York, we'd go out to hear some music.

One Monday night, we went to this club, and there was this Cuban band with four or five trombones; it just knocked me out. I wanted to do that. So I talked with Mark, and we put this band together called Bonerama. It was just a side project, and we started it in 1998. Whenever we were off, we'd play some shows, and we'd write some songs. The crazy thing was, it started catching on, and people were coming out and liking what we did! It was becoming a little more popular; we recorded three records.

Then the hurricane [Hurricane Katrina] happened, and everything went crazy. We recorded another record after that back in New Orleans. We got management for Bonerama, and we did a record with Harry at the same time. Then Harry was going to start another tour. We had our own shows going, so our manager sat us down and talked to us. We decided to leave Harry and focus on Bonerama, which was one of the best choices I could have made. I'm so glad I did it. It was wonderful being with Harry. We learned so much being with him. But it's always nice to have your own thing.

When we were with Harry's band, it was "Harry Connick, Jr. and His Band." You might get one solo a night, and some people didn't get any. I was lucky if I got one. But in our band, I can write my own songs, I can sing songs, and I can play as much as I want. Bonerama is going places where we dreamed it would go. It's really going there!

What drew you to the trombone?

I got started because I have an uncle who plays trombone. Jerry is six years older than I am, and about sixteen years younger than my mom, so we are closer in years, like brothers are. We still play together quite a bit. I started playing because he did. My grandmother would take me to go see him play. He would play in little jazz bands and stuff, and that was my first introduction. As happens quite often in a lot of places around the country, but especially in New Orleans, it seems that families are very influential on how other people grow up to play music. We have a lot of musical families here: The Nevilles, The Marsalises. It's quite common to have a family of musicians, and that was my introduction to it.

What drew you to jazz music?

I started out as a jazz musician because of the instrument that I play. But the band I'm playing in now, Bonerama, is not a jazz band. A rock/funk/brass band is what it is. Over the last few years, rock and funk have been as influential for me as jazz was in the past. I find myself listening to it more, and trying to listen to guitar players, and thinking, "You know what? Jimi Hendrix and Duane Allman are playing some stuff that I really like, and I want to learn how to play this stuff." I want to really get into what they are doing and apply it to the trombone.

The world is open. You don't have to be confined to one thing. I'm really glad where I am now with the band Bonerama because it's very interesting the way things are going, and how we apply this music to an instrument that people wouldn't even consider suitable for the music that we're doing.

Who played the most significant role in your musical development? Why?

Most of my influences are all New Orleans musicians, just because we are so lucky to have so many great musicians that most people may not even know about. As far as a trombone influence, there's a musician named Frog Joseph [Waldren "Frog" Joseph], who is the father of Kirk Joseph and Charles Joseph. Those were the guys who helped found the Dirty Dozen Brass Band. So hearing Frog, that was one of the biggest influences.

And there were a lot of traditional New Orleans musicians. The thing about New Orleans is, there is a lot of work. There are plenty of gigs for musicians, and plenty of places where musicians can play. So there is a lot of opportunity to go out and hear this music live. People go to schools, they go to colleges, they go to Berklee, and they go to Manhattan School of Music, or whatever. You can pay your tuition, and you can go to school, and you can transcribe solos, and do all of that stuff, but the real learning experience comes from getting out and hearing the musicians who have influenced you, playing live, and then getting a chance to talk with them and maybe play with them.

I was lucky enough to come across a lot of that. These guys were so open. It wasn't a competition thing; people are very friendly down here. The musicians were always very open and willing to talk about what they did, or give you some advice. Even just being around them was an influence.

What really stands out in my mind is that when I was in high school, from around 1974 to 1978, we would go down to the French Quarter. Everybody had fake IDs. At fifteen years old, my friends and I could get into bars at that time because New Orleans was just a wide-open kind of place. We would go to Pat O'Brien's and drink hurricanes. Preservation Hall was right next to Pat O'Brien's. I heard this music coming out of there, and it caught my attention. I would go back and get my hurricane, leave my friends at Pat O'Brien's, and go into Preservation Hall. In there, I was mesmerized by seeing these great musicians that were somewhat in their older age, in their fifties and sixties, but still in their prime. It was a really good time to hear this kind of music. That is what really caught my attention and kind of subliminally stood in my mind until I came back and reconnected to it in the early eighties, when I started hanging around with these brass bands.

Is the life that you are living bigger than the one you had envisioned for yourself?

I still have a vision of it being bigger and better. It's getting there. I didn't really have a plan until I started meeting some real musicians, like Leroy Jones and Lucien Barbarin, in the younger generation of musicians. I started seeing how they were approaching the music, and then I started having more a vision of, okay, this is what I want to do, and this is how I can go about doing it.

What have you learned about your character as a result of being in this business?

I realized that I believe in myself more and more as I go on. That I really can do something or play something or write something that may be significant, maybe at least to me. I realized that I can definitely make it as a musician. I don't doubt myself; I know that I can do it. Sometimes, it takes a lot of courage to realize that because it's not easy. It's really not easy. Trying just to be a musician and make a living, it's hard. Some guys do struggle with that. Maybe it discourages them from really going full-steam ahead and just doing it. Instead, they turn sideways and go this way and that way. I'm going straight ahead, and that's the only road that I see for me.

When you're not always motivated and not always playing your best, I have things to do that will move it along. Practicing more will help move it along. After the hurricane, everything just went crazy. My house flooded, and my family was in Baton Rouge [Louisiana], and I was between Baton Rouge and New Orleans. Sometimes it's a little bit harder to find time to spend writing or practicing. So at times, you get in and you do feel that lack of motivation.

Since the hurricane, I've felt it a little more because it's been harder to find spaces of time to really focus. But there are things that can be done. Practice really is something that you can't go wrong with. That's something that, as a musician, you have to do. You can't get by without practicing. There's no way. I don't think anybody can be a virtuoso or can even be a great musician without practicing. Louis Armstrong practiced. Everybody has to practice. There's no way of getting around it. Being a brass player, it's something you have to do every day. You really do. June Gardner, an old drummer from New Orleans, gave me some words of wisdom one time. He said, "You've got to treat your ax like you treat your wife—you've got to kiss it every day." If you don't do that, you lose it.

You mentally get down when you're not playing as well, too. Big time. That's the first thing that you feel. The mental definitely clogs things up a little. You start kind of doubting, but it's something that everybody goes through. I think it's something everybody goes through in any walk of life. You can overcome that. It's not hard to overcome it. Lately, I've discovered that yoga has helped a lot. That helps clear the mind a lot. And just trying to be a positive-thinking person, trying to use your subconscious mind to realize what your ultimate goal is, to stick with it and to not get detoured, so you can overcome those little blocks like that.

Was there anyone who said that you wouldn't be able to make it in the music business—what was your response to him or her?

No, not really.

Were there times when you thought that you might not make it yourself?

I did question myself. At first, I went through one semester majoring in music at Loyola University in New Orleans. I wasn't so much into it and sat out for a semester.

Then I decided to go back to school and went to a small school in Louisiana, about an hour outside of New Orleans, in Hammond, called Southeastern Louisiana University. I went through about three or four different majors, and it took me about six years to get out. I was on a very slow plan there! What happened was, I started playing music. While I majored in business there, I was also playing in a jazz band they had, a big band. I wanted to keep reading music; I didn't just want to let everything fall off. I still wanted to play; it was my passion. So when I was in school, I started getting gigs and driving back and forth to New Orleans. I had a gig on Wednesday nights, plus I had Friday and Saturday regular gigs. So I would drive in on Wednesdays, then drive back and go to class.

At that point, I was just starting to play and just getting my eyes open to really making money and playing gigs. Then my Uncle Jerry started bringing me around. He said, "Hey, you've got to come and march with this brass band called The Tumblers."

They would meet on Sundays, different times of the year,

at the Dream Palace in the French Quarter. They would do these parades through the Quarter and stop at bars. It was a pretty eye-opening experience because everybody would be in costume. It was almost like a parody of what the brass bands were. Half the people in the band really weren't musicians, and it would include dance teams. What they would call dance teams were the girls dancing in the front, and they would call them "The Poodles." It was ridiculous!

So, as I started doing that, I met some real musicians through Jerry, a couple of trumpet players and a tuba player. Out of that band started the Storyville Stompers Brass Band. That was when I started getting my real New Orleans education. These guys were into the Olympia Brass Band and real New Orleans music and brass bands, and also other types of New Orleans music. That was when I started seeing the real New Orleans culture that many people don't really see, like getting the chance to play at jazz funerals and second lines.

My family grew up in the city [New Orleans], and when I was in first grade, they moved to Metairie, the suburbs. So it was my chance to be involved in some real New Orleans stuff. That's kind of what really opened my eyes. Well, maybe I can, I thought. It might be possible to do this.

Now, I don't doubt myself. The switch came when I started playing with Harry. First, because it worked financially, I had a taste of a bit of success. I thought, okay, here's what it is supposed to taste like. I think that was definitely the turning point for me. Also, being around the level of musicians that are in that band, starting with Harry. Most people don't even realize how talented that guy is—he's unbelievable. People see the shows and they say, "Oh, he's talented." But being with him and seeing him in rehearsals and in the studio, I could see his talent come out. Being around people like that is very encouraging. It makes you want to strive to be better, in order to be around people like that. Those kinds of things inspire, or are supposed to inspire, you to move on and be better and dig in.

It did, and it still does, being around all these wonderful musicians that I'm blessed and lucky enough to be around. Like I said before, it's being in the right place at the right time and taking advantage of the situation.

What, for you, was the most unexpected aspect about being a professional musician?

It was all unexpected and continues to be so, in a good, positive way.

If you were able, at this point in your life, to leave a note for your younger self when you were just starting out, what would the note say?

It would say a lot of things like, good luck. Surround yourself with people who love what you do, and it will all turn out fine.

Do you have a favorite quote that inspires or motivates you?

I would say a favorite quote of mine is "It is what it is." That is the truth.

What does music mean to you?

Music is a very pleasing art. It can soothe the savage beast, and there are a lot of beasts to be soothed.

Freddy Cole

✦

Birthdate: October 15, 1931

Birthplace: Chicago

Main instruments: Vocals, piano

Website: www.freddycole.com

How long have you been a professional musician?

Since around the age of twelve or fourteen. I sang at a wedding and made twenty-five dollars. I thought I was rich!

Have you had to support yourself with other jobs, or has music been your only profession?

I've had two other jobs in my life, other than being a paperboy and cutting grass when I was a kid. As a teen, I worked at the Great Lakes Naval Training Center. I also worked at The Storkline Furniture store, which was the last non-music job I ever had, at around age eighteen or nineteen.

Life has been good to me; music has been good to me. I can't complain, not one bit! I've been lucky; I've been blessed.

What drew you to the piano?

That's a good question because I don't know. I just started to play. I was very young—four, five, six years old—somewhere in there. As long as I can remember, I've been singing and playing piano. I don't know which came first.

What drew you to jazz music?

Jazz music has been around me all of my life. When that's something that you always hear, and you grow up around it, then it just becomes an everyday part of you.

Who played the most significant role in your musical development? Why?

So many people, I wouldn't know where to begin. I've been lucky enough to grow up around so many outstanding musicians, and, of course, my brothers [Eddie, Ike and Nat], as well. It's just difficult for me to start naming names because I'm sure I would miss someone along the way!

I would say it was a collaboration of wonderful musicians. A lot of people know them as great musicians and would be in awe of them, but I wasn't because I saw them all the time.

Sonny Greer, who was a drummer with Duke Ellington's band, is one example. How much he meant to me when I was a youngster in New York trying to find my way; he was a great mentor. Guys like him and many, many others like Milt Hinton and Osie Johnson. They used to call me "Little Cole." All of them knew my brother [Nat King Cole]. When they would see me going astray, they would sit me down and talk to me, which was very beneficial to my learning this business and in

FREDDY'S MUSICAL NOTES

♪ Freddy has been nominated for a Grammy three times: in 2011, for *Freddy Cole Sings Mr. B* (High-Note Records, 2010); in 2009, for his album *Music Maestro Please* (HighNote Records, 2008); and again in 2007, for his album *Because of You* (High-Note Records, 2006).

♪ In 2007, he was inducted into the Georgia Hall of Fame.

♪ Freddy was added to the Steinway Artist roster in 2006.

♪ His musical family includes his brothers Eddie, Ike, and Nat, sister Evelyn, and niece Natalie.

learning how to be professional. I owe an awful lot of that to Mr. Sonny Greer.

Is the life that you are living bigger than the one you had envisioned for yourself?

Not really, I never set big goals. I always lived one day at a time. The way that I'm living right now, and have been over the years, is due to the fact that I am just plowing right along.

I enjoyed the competition out on the New York streets. I look back on it now, and it was a great experience to have come through that—the days when you just had a gig, or you were playing here or there, and then you had to ride the subway for eight hours to get somewhere else in New York. You had a little hall room where you were playing for eight dollars a week, or for eleven dollars a week. And now I can sit here and look out my window at land and all kind of trees—it's beautiful! What can I say? I'm blessed!

What have you learned about your character as a result of being in this business?

Your character gets tested quite often. One thing I learned about character was from my father, my brother Nat, and my older brother Ike. They had a lot of character—if they told you something, that was it. I've learned to live by that rule. If I tell you I'm going to do something, I do it.

I know people who make a statement just to be making a statement—they have no intention of following up on it. It's like a person who will tell a lie when the truth will do. It means a lot to your wellbeing to have good character.

Was there anyone who said that you wouldn't be able to make it in the music business—what was your response to him or her?

Yes, there were—they just didn't come right out and tell you. That's one of the great joys that I get now at this point in my life—to look back at those who looked down on you. I don't carry grudges because that's just too much of a burden. To be carrying around with you, "I don't like this guy because he did this or he did that," is just too difficult.

The greatest thing that happened to you was that you overcame it all.

Now they come running to me. They say, "Oh, I love that new CD of yours." Or, "I knew you would make it." I just say, "Fine, thank you so much, I'm glad that you're happy," and you move on. Why hold a grudge? For what? It's only hurting you; it's not hurting them. If you can't see, you can't grow.

Were there times when you thought that you might not make it yourself?

No, I never did. One thing that I learned over the years that has been very beneficial to me is that if you can't stand rejection, don't get in this business. Do something else! Sell cars or get a job.

What, for you, was the most unexpected aspect of being a professional musician?

I would have to say it was dealing with some people in the management part of the business. I was raised to respect people, which I always do. But then some people can be so conniving and cutthroat. I look back at some of those people, though some of them have helped me along the way, of course; I can't say they didn't. To see them nowadays, it would really give you great joy from smashing a pie in their faces! But I feel better knowing that I can smile instead and say, "How are you doing? I hope all is well with you." That was an unexpected part of the business that I really didn't enjoy.

If you were able, at this point in your life, to leave a note for your younger self when you were just starting out, what would the note say?

Have fun! Live the life. I've lived a great life. If he can have half as much fun as I've had, he'll be in good shape.

Do you have a favorite quote that inspires or motivates you?

One thing I would say is a quotation from [Ralph Waldo] Emerson: "To envy is ignorant." All I do is what concerns me, and I don't worry what people think.

What does music mean to you?

Everything. I can't go to sleep without music. Music is playing at my house all the time, twenty-four hours a day. It's just all around me, and it's been good to me. I wish I could be half as good to music as it has been to me.

Mindi Abair

Birthdate: May 31, 1969

Birthplace: St. Petersburg, Florida

Main instruments: Vocals, alto and soprano saxophone

Website: www.mindiabair.com

How long have you been a professional musician?

I had my first paying gig when I was in college, at eighteen years old. I actually saved a photocopy of the check; I got paid fifty dollars. It was at a Chinese restaurant, and I was playing with a singer/songwriter. I remember she was playing a bunch of cool stuff, and I was playing along with her on sax. Then she decided to play "Puff the Magic Dragon."

I just thought to myself, "Wow! I need to lead these gigs. This is not cool. But I am getting paid, so shut up and play 'Puff the Magic Dragon'!" That was another stimulus for me to start my own band.

I had many day jobs to make a living. Through college, I played probably six nights a week with different bands. I was in a fusion band, and I was in a pop band where we would go out and do Top 40 stuff. For the songs I didn't know the words to, I would play sax, so it worked out pretty well. I would play with so many different bands, and that was definitely a part of coming up the ranks. Not only am I getting paid for it and finding out what the business is like, but just being out there night after night and kind of finding yourself with your instrument—that was invaluable.

You hear from all these older musicians, "You got to cut your teeth; you got to get out there and play six nights a week, five sets a night." They're right, and I was a different person for it, for sure.

Have you had to support yourself with other jobs, or has music been your only profession?

When I came to L.A., I immediately got a job as a waitress because no one would hire me as a musician. I would walk into jam sessions in Los Angeles and ask if I could play. They wouldn't even think I was a musician. I looked like a cheerleader, at that point. I was twenty-one years old, and I'm sure I didn't look the part of what I was trying to be. It was interesting. I learned you kind of have to make your own.

And because no one would hire me, I made my own. I did everything from playing on the street to pay the rent, to booking myself as a solo saxophonist, and playing in lobbies of hotels or parties. I even played with a trio, or a duo, and hired guys I wanted to play with. Whatever they wanted, that's what I had.

I begged my friend from college at Berklee, in Boston, Tommy Coster, Jr., to move to L.A. because I didn't know anyone here who would play with me. I promised him I would get us bookings. He moved to L.A. from Boston, and I did get us bookings. We did the coffee shop circuit and played basically anywhere they would feed us dinner!

After that, he helped me get guys to play with us, and, between us, we formed my first band. I played all the little dirty

MINDI'S MUSICAL NOTES

♪ Mindi is an elected governor for the Los Angeles Chapter of National Academy of Recording Arts and Sciences (NARAS) for the 2010-2012 term, and is an Artist Ambassador for Campbell's Labels for Education and The Grammy Foundation.

♪ In 2011, she appeared as herself, playing sax in the bar, in the Fran Drescher sitcom, *Happily Divorced.*

♪ In 2010, Mindi was featured on *American Idol* twice, with Casey Abraham and Paul McDonald.

♪ At age seven, she went to charm school at Sears.

rocker clubs in Hollywood, and any jazz club or restaurant that would let us in. Everyone was playing for free. We moved up slowly to getting paid maybe thirty dollars to fifty dollars a night. We definitely paid our dues. We even played on the route of the L.A. Marathon (for free), just to play. We didn't say no to any moneymaking opportunity or any opportunity to get in front of people and play. You never know.

At one point, I was playing on the street alone in Santa Monica, and Bobby Lyle walked past me. He is a veteran jazz musician. He is incredible, and I recognized him immediately, since I was already a fan. He walked by and stood and watched me play for a while.

I am thinking to myself, "I've got a college education, and I am out here on the street playing, and I've got Bobby Lyle watching me. This is a little embarrassing."

He stayed to the end of the song, and then he walked up and said, "You are really good. I should hire you for something."

And I thought, "Well, maybe this isn't embarrassing. Maybe this is pretty cool."

He did hire me, and I played on one of his albums, *Power of Touch* [Atlantic/WEA, 1997], and toured with him on and off for years.

We'll still do stuff together every once in a while. He was a huge part of my coming up the ranks. It all came from his walking up Third Street Promenade in Santa Monica and seeing me out there with my case out.

What drew you to the saxophone?

I grew up on the road with my dad's band. My dad [musician Lance Abair] was in a band called The Entertainers. From the time I was born, until I was about five, we didn't have a house. We just traveled. It was my mom, my dad, me, and the band. A few other people in the band had kids. We just moved from place to place. What a crazy way to grow up, in theory, but I thought it was really fun! Just being able to be around music and musicians, and get to adapt to different places and enjoy different places, was a great way to grow up. Even looking back, I think, "Wow, what an experience!"

We moved to Florida after his band broke up, and I went into school. My dad started me with piano lessons at age five. School band started when I got into fourth grade, when I was eight years old. The band teacher just put a bunch of instruments down on the floor in the middle of the band class and said, "Take the next few minutes and choose an instrument you like. Go around, look at them, and see what appeals to you. Once you find one, take it and sit down."

I looked at the sax and thought, "I've watched my dad on stage for so many years playing sax." He was the kind that would run around and have a good time and play. He was the coolest guy I knew, at eight years old. So, I took the sax and thought I'd have as much fun as it looked like he was having.

Sure enough, it worked out. No one told me it was odd for a girl to play sax until it was way too late, which I applaud them for. I just kept going with it, and I had so much fun with it.

To me, the saxophone is the closest instrument to the human voice. You can do things with a saxophone. You can scream and you can whine and you can emote. It has incredible power. It's an instrument that definitely became an extension of me.

When I play the piano, it is very shape-driven. I write a lot on the piano. But it has one sound—you press a note and you are going to get that sound. The thing that really brought me in with saxophone was that you can get so many different sounds. It is like a voice, except with more possibility.

I will never feel like I am a master of any of it; you keep trying to find yourself and create different things. Anything with music is a journey, and it is a life journey. I think that is part of the fun of it.

Each year, I write with some of my friends, and we always push each other. It's like, "I know who you are; I know what you can do. Surprise me. Go further. Push yourself to be better."

Every record we do, we push each other, saying, "You know what? That's not good enough. It sounds like it could have been on the last record. No, we are moving forward; we are going to bring out new parts of each other. We are going to say something different."

You are always going to be yourself, but to push yourself to learn more, to constantly be better—sometimes it works; sometimes it doesn't—but that is always my goal.

What drew you to jazz music?

If you play the saxophone for any length of time, you have to come across jazz at some point. It is inescapable; jazz is the history of saxophone. I grew up hearing Clarence Clemons rock with Bruce Springsteen. I loved him. I heard Maceo Parker with James Brown. He was the funkiest!

But at a certain point, I heard these jazz players, and I thought, "Wow, the saxophone can do that! That's really cool." So I started delving into it. At the time I was getting into it, my dad had all these old records. I figured he was my dad, so his record collection couldn't be too hip. Little did I know.

Then I got into college, and my new friends in college asked, "Do you like traditional jazz, or do you like contemporary jazz?" I didn't know the difference. I had just heard a couple of jazz artists in passing, really. I had heard David Sanborn and the Yellowjackets in high school. I thought they were amazing. I was a huge fan of both, but I didn't really know what traditional versus contemporary jazz was.

So, we started to sit down, and they would play me all these records, and it opened the door to all this new music. I started buying every Miles Davis record, and every [John] Coltrane record and every Wayne Shorter and Cannonball Adderley record. All of a sudden, my dad's record collection looked really incredible! My mind changed; he really was cool, wasn't he?

I loved jazz all through college; that's all I really listened to during that period of time. I immersed myself in it, and I became so in love with it. When I started to write my own music, which was early on in college, it was a mix of all the pop and rock that I had grown up listening to but mixed in with some cool jazz chords that I was just starting to learn, and some melodic ideas that were more jazz-influenced. The metamorphosis was just starting. Even now, as someone who's written a lot of music and has five jazz CDs on major labels, I still don't consider myself traditional or holding to the tradition of jazz that Charlie Parker or Dizzy Gillespie held to, but it's my own brand. It's the pop and rock and soul that I grew up with, along with the jazz that I fell in love with in college.

For me, the people who were in jazz were the rock stars of their time; they were the cool guys breaking the rules and playing stuff that other people weren't playing. That's definitely Miles Davis—he just kept changing and morphing, much to people's dismay, at some points. But it made me happy. He would strive for change and strive to make himself better. He would take what was in the day's music and find himself in it. He was never happy with the status quo; he was always trying to one-up himself and constantly search for a new sound.

So for me, I am never shy about leaning towards different styles of music, whether I'm writing or playing. I'm not scared to do it because I watched Miles Davis change and morph, and I was so inspired by his doing that. I think that's more than allowed in the jazz world. I don't think that they would look at themselves as making the rules of jazz; I think they would be the guys going, "No, put a funky beat behind that melody, or put in some minor seventh chords with a rock beat. Try it! See how it goes." That's how I view it, so that's how I'm doing it. It's what appeals to me.

I studied saxophone with Joe Viola at Berklee College of Music. It was a great school, but the school is only as good as its teachers. Week after week, I would go into his office, and he would say, "I want you to start your own band. I want you to do your own music. I know you write a lot and you've got your own sound. You should go after that. Don't try to be the next so and so. Don't try to play like your friends; don't try to play like Coltrane. Don't try to be Cannonball Adderley, or Maceo, or Charlie Parker."

These were the people who, in school, we idolized. We would all sit and play John Coltrane transcriptions and play along to the records of different people, whether it was David Sanborn or Wayne Shorter.

I think that was a nice lesson to be told—don't try to be them. Be yourself. He actually let me play a concert with my own band (that he'd pushed me to create for a while) for my senior recital. That was a huge turning point for me because I had to put together a whole concert, play my own music, and be the leader, plus believe that I had a sound worthy of people hearing. That was an incredible step for me. I started realizing that I should go after my own sound and what's in my own head, instead of being the next David Sanborn, or the next Michael Brecker or Cannonball Adderley. Create your own world, and then you've got a shot.

Who played the most significant role in your musical development? Why?

I think Stevie Wonder is one of the reasons I phrase the way I do, or I play the way I do. I played along to so many of his harmonica solos and so many of his vocal lines. I just loved the way he played and the way he sang.

Rickie Lee Jones inspired me. I had such immense respect for her, musically. I love artists who are themselves, and when you hear them you think, "How did they come up with that?" Rickie Lee Jones was such a huge vocal influence for me. I loved that she sounded like a horn player because she would put these vocal parts together, and I would think, "That is something I do as a sax player, with complex tight voicings and cluster chords." But she'd sing it, and she'd sing it like a horn playing, with the phrasing and stuff, and I thought, "No one else is doing that! How did she come up with that?"

As a kid, growing up and listening to my father and the people he recorded with was a huge learning curve for me. I would always just listen. Sometimes, you don't need lessons from someone. You just listen to who they are, and you try to become that, or you just become it. My father was a huge early influence. He'd let me sit in on his sessions and play, from the time I was about ten years old. He had a great big sound on alto saxophone, and I wanted that. My approach to sound is very similar to his; I love his sound.

I never really had private music teachers until I was in college. I just found my own way. There were people that I looked up to early on, and I would try to pattern myself after them. As a kid, it was all the pop and rock people. I thought Blondie was the coolest thing going. She was strong, and she was cool, and she would just walk out there on stage and own it.

Madonna was a strong female role model, the fact that she would go out there and show the guys how it was done. She was unapologetic; she wanted to take over the world. One of my favorite performers has always been Tina Turner. She just goes out there and gives one thousand percent; she never stops. I loved her intensity and showmanship. I wanted to do that on saxophone.

Also, Joni Mitchell was a big influence. She would just choose people in her band who added so much to her. She had this amazing personality and so much to say as an artist, and she hired people who also had so much to say. Records like *Shadows and Light* [Elektra/WEA, 1980] show the coming together of such great musicians along with her. She showed me that it doesn't have to be just about you; it can be about incredible musicians coming together and making more out of your music and taking it further. I loved that. I still write with my friends and still hire people for my band that I believe have such incredible character in and of themselves. They make me look good.

I was hugely inspired by Miles Davis, as well. I own a lot of the records he made, though not all because that's just impossible! Every incarnation of his is like going to school for me. He chose people who were incredible to both play and write with. I think they changed who he was, and he changed who they were. I always strive to be that artist: to take a snapshot of what I'm feeling musically, mix it with people whom I respect and love for what they add musically, and make a record or go out and create it live every night.

The people that I toured with, early on, were huge influences. I think that would probably be overlooked, mostly, but I toured with a lot of different people on the way up. All I wanted to be was a solo artist, but no record label wanted to sign me. It's a hard thing to get signed to a record label and be able to make your own records, so coming up the ranks, I played with a bunch of different artists.

I went on the road for over a year with the Backstreet Boys for their Millennium Tour. I played keyboards, percussion and saxophone. We played to fifty- to sixty-thousand screaming girls every night. It was absolutely bigger than life. And it was an incredible life experience. I got to run around and play extended solos while they changed clothes. It was an amazing thing to be a part of.

Then I put together Mandy Moore's first band and played with her for a couple of years. I played keyboards and sang and played percussion for her.

I toured and recorded with Adam Sandler. I learned a lot from him. I had just come out of college and was still in a very heady mindset. I was thinking about what chord substitutions would be hip over what changes—very jazz-minded. Adam just wanted to rock. And his band was a bunch of veteran rockers, as well. I learned that sometimes it's not about thinking. It's just about rocking out and having fun.

I played with Duran Duran's comeback to America; that was total rock-stardom. And I respected Nick [Rhodes] so much (and had to laugh, too) because he cared just as much about what I was wearing as what I was going to play over the song. John Taylor is a great friend and has been on most of my CDs. He's an incredible musician and just an all-around inspiring person. He co-wrote "It Just Happens That Way" [*It Just Happens That Way,* Verve, 2003], and played with me on it. He also sang with me on "Save Tonight" [*It Just Happens That Way,* Verve, 2003]. And we co-wrote "F.L.A. Swing" [*Stars,* Peak Records, 2008] together. I get the chance to play with Duran Duran every once in a while now, though not often enough.

I toured with Tina Marie for a little while—total R&B, just a completely different avenue of thought. I loved playing her music; what a deep groove you get to sink into.

Jazz artists like John Tesh, or Jonathan Butler, or Bobby Lyle—all of those people had such different music to learn and to delve into. As a player, I delved into it! I had to learn their music, and I had to play it right every night. It had to become a part of me. I've got to say, as an artist, I really think that helped me.

I think I am the sum of my influences. I took from every one of those situations, learning those people's music and playing it night after night. I really think it helped me find what I had to say as an artist. I love that. I figured I was getting paid to see the world, but I never thought it would help me find me. But by the end, I was thinking I was a really different person, a really different player—someone who's a little deeper, a little wiser. I didn't see that coming. I think even the little things that you don't plan on being important in your life can make a huge difference in the end.

Is the life that you are living bigger than the one you had envisioned for yourself?

I get asked in interviews all the time, "So where are you going from here? What's next?" I usually say, "What I'm doing right now is what I've always dreamed of doing." It's pretty amazing: I walk onstage every night with my band, and I get to play the music that I've written and that has meaning for me. That is the best thing in the world to be able to do. As a kid, that's what I dreamed of doing. I want to go out, I want to have my band, and I want to make records.

My mom and dad were moving a few years ago and my mom dug up an admission form I had done to get into college. I had to write a letter saying how I saw my life. It asked, "What do you see yourself doing in twenty years?"

I had written, "By the time twenty years hits, I will have had a few records on a major label with my band, playing my music. I'll be touring the country." It was exact, even down to the point where "and when I'm not on tour with my band, I'll probably be renovating my house." Now, literally, that's what I do. I come home from tour, and I say, "Hey, let's pull apart the bathroom and change it!"

It is funny that as a kid, I had a really clear vision of who I wanted to be. I don't think I knew what style of music I would necessarily go towards because I just liked to play and to write. I didn't really have a strong view of where I was going to end up, but I knew I wanted to go out and play. So I am pretty much exactly where I wanted to be.

I came to L.A., and it definitely wasn't easy, but for every door that was closed, I would try to find a hallway to another door, or try to find a way to do what I wanted to do. It wasn't easy, and there were definitely points where I thought, "Okay, maybe I'm nuts! Maybe I should just go do what my other high school friends did, and start a family and get a normal job, and that kind of stuff." But it was so in my heart to go and play and be out there, to go have fun playing music, that I would just find any way to make it happen!

Today, I am having a blast! I get to make my own records, and I get to make them with my friends, which is amazing. I get to go to the studio, have lunch with my friend, and sit and talk about life. We'll write a song, figure out what to do with it, and how to make that vision come to reality. Then I bring in my friends to play on the record. What a fun thing to do! I absolutely don't take it for granted. I don't really need anything else to be happy, in my professional life. If I get to keep doing this for the rest of my life—all is good!

I did really have to work hard and try to make a place for myself, but I did. People told me, "You can't do that," or, "That's not possible." But I survived, and I think that's something to be proud of. Maybe I'm stronger than I thought I was, as a kid. I've kind of weathered storms and got through them without getting too crazy! It lets me know that if there's something I want to do, I've got the strength to make it happen, if I really want it. That's a nice thing—to believe in yourself.

I've seen myself fight to make stuff happen and fight to get different places and play. I definitely came from humble beginnings; no one handed me anything. My dad didn't know the record industry, and he didn't know someone to call to get me signed to a label. He would have made a call if he did! I grew up in a very small town [St. Petersburg, Florida]. If I had grown up in Los Angeles, maybe I would have been a solo artist a lot earlier, had it a lot easier, and would have known the right people to make things happen quickly. But I look back on the journey and think it's pretty amazing.

What have you learned about your character as a result of being in this business?

My dad was a musician, but he would never teach me music. My dad played sax and keyboards and bass—he played basically anything that was in front of him. His mother was an opera singer. Later in her life, she taught piano and vocals. Neither one of them would teach me how to play or sing. They didn't want to be that person who would push me, and then one day find I would hate them for it. There is that day in every kid's life when you hate your music teacher. So I had both of these people who were huge musical influences and inspirations. They'd play and sing with me, and my dad would let me hang out in the studio. Even though they wouldn't teach me, they were really supportive. They let me find my love of music on my own, so it was mine. I love them for that.

There's an early story that I look back on and think, "Thank God I learned that early." I had this huge audition—in my mind, it was huge. It was for the Florida All-State Jazz Band. Every year they put together a band of students. They have a wind ensemble, a jazz band, and a symphonic band. I wanted to be in the jazz band because I thought that was where the "cool" kids hung out.

I practiced and practiced for the audition and finally came to the conclusion that I was not good enough. I had heard kids in the All-State jazz band just really play. They were good, and I was new to it. I didn't grow up playing over changes; I grew up listening to Top 40 radio. At that point, I was the only person in our school who would stand up and take a solo in our jazz band, not because I was good, but because I had the guts to stand up not knowing what I was doing and still play! It was either sheer guts, or sheer ignorance.

So, I gave up practicing for my audition. I put my sax down, and I went to my dad and said, "These guys are going to eat me alive, and I'm not going to go to this audition. So many people are better than me. I'm going to save myself the heart-break."

He said, "Okay, you can quit. That's fine." Of course, he knew my personality, when he said I could quit.

I said, "Well, I don't want to quit, but you know...."

He said, "No, no, it's fine; go ahead and quit."

So his reverse psychology worked, and I did the audition. I won the first chair alto saxophone for the Florida All-State Jazz Band. I came home, and I was jumping up and down, saying, "Oh, my gosh, I got it! I can't believe I got it!"

He just looked at me and said, "You know what? Sometimes it's not about who is the best, or who is the most talented, or any of that. Sometimes it's just about going after your dream. It's about going after something you want. There are a bunch of talented people who either won't put in the work, or they won't believe enough in themselves to even try. People who go after it have a shot."

That's the best lesson. Sometimes it really is about going out and doing what you love and putting your best foot forward.

You wonder if anyone's road is easy. And whether you choose to be a car mechanic or work in an office, it's got its ups and downs. The music business certainly has its share of hardships, and it takes a lot of work to get there. But it is something that if, as a child, you are inclined towards music and your heart is in music, is definitely worth the trip. It's worth putting up the fight and making the sacrifice and going for it.

Was there anyone who said that you wouldn't be able to make it in the music business—what was your response to him or her?

Sure, of course. I remember the mother of one of my friends in high school said, "This isn't a real possibility. Girls don't go out and become musicians for a living. So you really need to sit down and come up with something that is more acceptable."

I looked at her and said, "I don't want to do anything else. I've done it up to this point, and it's been fine. I just think I kind of have to make my own."

She said, "Well, it's just not done." So I didn't try to tell her she was wrong. I understood that it was something that she just didn't think was acceptable for a young woman to do. But sometimes you've got to break the rules and do things your own way!

I just kind of went out there and tried. Many people along the way said, "Oh, that's impossible! You can't move to L.A.—that's such a huge town. What will you do, when you don't know anyone?" I thought, "Well, you know, I'll figure it out."

So, with all the "No's," I just figured I would find a way to prove them wrong. Maybe that's all you need: someone that you want to prove wrong. You can't do it! Yeah, watch me! Anyone who said I couldn't, I just thought, "Well, we'll see. I'm going to go out there and give it my best shot."

This is what fuels me; this is what gets me up in the morning; this is what I look forward to. If there's any chance at making a living with something that you look forward to and something that inspires you, you should give it every chance, I think.

My mom went to an office every day to work, and she told me, "I hope you don't become like me. I hope you go out and go after your dreams. I go to a job that I don't love, every day. But I have to. And that's fine; I understand that's what life is. But I want you to be able to go after your dream."

That was something I was able to do because they were supportive of my doing that. Again, I think you go after what you love. If it doesn't work, okay, fine. But at least you have to go for it.

I'm definitely fueled by people telling me I can't do something. In 2010, I was elected as a governor for the Los Angeles chapter of The Recording Academy. They asked me in an interview what my secret to success was, and I responded that a lot of people had told me, "You can't." That just makes me want to do whatever it is even more!

Were there times when you thought that you might not make it yourself?

I've always believed in myself. I had really supportive parents growing up, and I have great friends and family around me now. I believed my teachers and family when I was a kid and they told me, "You can do anything you put your mind to." Life doesn't always take the path you think it'll take, but if you keep working towards what you want and doing what's in your heart, you'll have a pretty interesting journey, if nothing else!

What, for you, was the most unexpected aspect about being a professional musician?

I did have a lot of people early on tell me that being a woman in this industry was going to be a huge handicap, that I was going to have to work extra hard and all this stuff. Now, I don't disagree with them at this point. You do have to prove yourself more as a woman because people don't expect as much, I think. If I walk on stage, people aren't expecting me to sound as good, being a female instrumentalist.

One night, I was playing a concert in Seattle with Jonathan Butler, who is a black South African jazz and R&B artist. My mom and dad were in the audience. I walked on stage in the middle of his first song to play a solo and stayed to play with him. As I walked on, this girl sitting next to my mom said, "What is that skinny little white bitch doing on stage?" The perception was, it was going to be bad. But then, after I finished playing and we ended the song, the girl stood up on her feet and cheered for me. She said, "You go, you skinny little white bitch! You go!" She was my biggest fan!

For me, one of the most enjoyable parts is playing for people who have never seen my band, or seen me on stage, and trying to win them over. I love the fact that there are some strong women out there changing people's minds and holding up the torch, saying, "Hey, this is a new millennium; women can do anything."

If you were able, at this point in your life, to leave a note for your younger self when you were just starting out, what would the note say?

Definitely you get wiser, as you go through things and learn. Maybe I could have cut a few of the bunny trails getting to where I am. Maybe I would have just left a note that said, "Enjoy what's in front of you." So many times, I'd be waitressing or working for an office somewhere—I had varying odd jobs when I first came to L.A.—and I was so desperate to get into music or to play with anyone and just get out there.

It was a lot of pressure that I would put on myself. Even when my band was performing, I'd be nervous out there, thinking, "Oh, people are listening to us—I hope we are good enough," or that kind of stuff.

Maybe I'd say to just sit back and enjoy it more, and not be so anxious about the outcome, or worry too much. "You're gonna be alright. Just go out there and have a good time with it." Which I did, but I was always thinking, "Are we doing the right things?" You worry, and you want to do well when you're very young. You're just looking towards that carrot. As a kid, you want to do everything to be perfect, and you want everything to happen magically, but it doesn't. So you're always nervous that you should be doing this or that, but probably it wouldn't hurt to just sit back and enjoy what you're doing every second, regardless of the outcome.

Do you have a favorite quote that inspires or motivates you?

I have a cocktail napkin from a party that I stuffed in my pocket, and I have had it on my desk for a few years. It has this girl on it in this crazy outfit from the turn of the century. It says, "Be yourself; everyone else is already taken." It's a quote from Oscar Wilde. Those are good words to live by.

That's always been a theme in my music. I have an album called *Come as You Are* [GRP Records, 1994], and my first album was named *It Just Happens That Way* [Verve, 2003], which is a piece of a quote from a *Cannonball Adderly In New York: Live* [OJC, 1962] record that he did. He was basically saying he wanted to record a live album in front of a real jazz audience, an audience that "got it." Some people try to pretend like they are hip, and they want to go and see jazz and feel like they're cool. But you can't make coolness happen; it just happens that way. You either are cool, or you aren't.

What does music mean to you?

Music has always been in my life. It has always been part of who I was even before I played. I would listen to my grandmother sing, or I would listen to my dad play. I'd listen to music with my friends and dance in their rooms to it.

I wrote a song on my last record called "On and On" [*Stars*, Peak Records, 2008]. As I get older, I look back and think, "Wow, we were just kids getting together to sing in someone's garage, or go dance to whatever record my friend had bought." We took it for granted; that was what was fun. And now, this is what I do for a living. The lyrics to the song are: "On and on, the music plays; on and on."

Looking back, the music has always been the thread of my life. What a beautiful thing. It's something that has always been there with me, whether I am playing or just listening. It's always surrounded me, or been inside me, somehow.

Josh Brown

＋

Birthdate: September 3, 1973

Birthplace: Oakville, Ontario, Canada

Main instrument: Trombone

Other instruments: Euphonium, tuba, singing in the shower

Website: www.joshbrownjazz.com

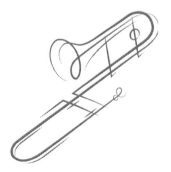

How long have you been a professional musician?

Ever since I finished college I have been actively playing professionally, and by that I mean supporting myself by playing music. So it has been about thirteen years.

My first paid gig was when I was thirteen, and that actually became a recurring gig for me. It was great. It was for Easter services at a church in my hometown. Every Easter, we'd play, and I'd make a hundred bucks a service. I was like, "Wow! I get to make money at this!" It never occurred to me that people got paid for this sort of thing.

Have you had to support yourself with other jobs, or has music been your only profession?

Being out of high school was probably the last time I had a regular day job. In college I supported myself somewhat by playing gigs and doing the odd job in the summer.

What drew you to playing the trombone?

Originally I had wanted to play the tuba. My career path would have definitely been different! In my town of Burlington, Ontario, we had a fantastic city marching band. They were, and still are, very, very good. They tour and play all over the world. When I was growing up, that was always around.

When I was eleven or twelve, I got to go in and choose which instrument I wanted. I really wanted to play drums. My father was a drummer when he was younger, and my mom taught piano at the house. So I don't know why I had this very strange, childlike battle in my head that I thought my mom would be disappointed because she dealt with actual notes, and drums don't have notes so much. I said, "Well, I guess

I'll play an instrument that actually has notes to it." So, for some reason, I liked the big marching sousaphone, those big things that wrap around your body. I said, "Well, I'll play that."

I remember coming home from school, and there was a concert tuba waiting for me in the living room. Of course, they look completely different, and I thought, what the hell is this? This isn't the tuba I want to play. I want the big one! So playing the tuba only lasted for about a week because it really didn't fit very well in the car, and I was probably a little small. So, they wound up sticking me with a euphonium, which is basically a mini-tuba. I ended up playing that all the way through high school. (Sadly, I never got the sousaphone.)

Fortunately, when I was around fourteen or fifteen, I had a wonderful teacher named George Behr, who saw that I had a

JOSH'S MUSICAL NOTES

♪ Josh was nominated as the Jazz Trombonist of the Year at the 2003 National Jazz Awards in Canada, his native country.

♪ He received the highest mark in the Royal Conservatory of Music's curriculum across Canada, which led to his hometown of Burlington, Ontario, giving him a Civic Recognition Award.

♪ One of his favorite things to do, when not playing trombone, is watching (and crying along with) romantic movies. Favorites include *You've Got Mail, An Affair to Remember,* and many other classics.

♪ In the Michael Bublé band, Josh is the current unbeaten champion in Mario Kart, though he admits he is no longer the best player.

tendency towards jazz. There pretty much aren't any jazz euphonium players that I can think of. It has the same mouthpiece, range, and timbre as the trombone. He was a trombone teacher, and he said, "It would be an easy switch for you, if you are interested in jazz, to pick up the trombone." I ended up playing both of them side by side all the way through high school and would just switch off between them given whatever circumstance I was in. So that's how I came upon the trombone. It was the third instrument after the first lowly week of tuba.

What drew you to jazz music?

Jazz was always on the radio in the house, but as a young musician, I think I was drawn to the syncopated nature of the music, the rhythm and the energy it created.

Who played the most significant role in your musical development? Why?

I was fortunate to have many good teachers, George Behr, Mike Polci, and Al Kay among others, but one in particular is Marc Donatelle. He'd come up from Chicago, and he was playing in the Hamilton Philharmonic, which is in the city just beside mine. It actually, at the time, had an orchestra but since has lost it. I had met him when I was doing the Royal Conservatory of Music, which is a cross-Canada competition. I was doing a lot of classical competitions at the time. He was a judge at one of the competitions, and my mom sort of got him to start teaching me. She was just trying to find me a teacher on a different level.

Marc was the first teacher that I met who was really, really into music. You could feel the excitement when he described phrases or musical pieces. He was just really animated. That made a big impression on me. Not to mention, he was just a phenomenal trombone player, just really, really great. He used to say things to me, not just solely about music, but about life in general, or about the life of being a musician. He'd tell me things that could be geared towards any sort of creative field or any job, really. I remember him telling me once that I'd better have a thick skin, if I'm going to be in the music business. Marc would go to an audition, and the people would say, "Well, you are a nice player, but you play too loud." Then he would go to the next audition, and the people would say, "You're a great player, but you play too soft." Basically, what he was saying is that it is all based on what someone thinks, and you can't let that get to you. You do what you do, and you've got to have a thick skin because this is a tough business. And he was definitely right! You've just got to do your thing and realize everyone's a critic, and everyone's going to have their opinion about you. I was seventeen, eighteen, and to get that sort of information at that age went far beyond anyone just teaching me the basic mechanics. What he told me are things that I am still dealing with, even now. These are everyday things that still occur.

I had some really great high school teachers, nothing but support from my parents on every level, and even some fantastic college teachers. But some things that Marc said to me were basically the right stuff at the right time, at that age. I was fortunate that my playing came easily for me, and I was more interested in doing things like wind surfing and stuff like that. He showed me that you have to do a lot of work, first of all. And if you should go down that path, here's what you'll deal with. And if you are wanting to go forth, just be aware of these facts. So now, when I do clinics and things like that, I don't just go and tell kids what they want to hear, I lay it out for them. This is a tough life, so if you really want it, go for it. But realize—not that there's any security in any other line of work these days—there's definitely no security in music! There's no health plan, there's no retirement plan. It may all seem great now, but twenty years down the road, you'll be like, "Hmmm. Okay. Now what?" This is real life. Playing music is such a unique and amazing thing, and you don't want to detract from the enthusiasm, especially when you talk to little kids. Music is supposed to be fun. And if it's not fun for you, don't do it. Ultimately, it can become a deep, meaningful experience, but on the surface of it, it should just be fun. And if it stops being fun, then you shouldn't do it—because there are definitely easier ways to make a buck!

But, I've been fortunate. Through doing this, I've been around the world, had incredible, unique experiences and have met amazing people I would never have met, had I had a different career. In many ways, I'm just a much better person for having been through this. And it's not like my journey is done. Every day is different. This is, hopefully for me, a lifelong career. I have that goal in sight. I always want to play music; it isn't just an "of the moment" thing. This is what I do. This is what I've always loved to do. And, hopefully, I'll always get to do it.

Is the life that you are living bigger than the one you had envisioned for yourself?

I could never have imagined what I am doing now, back then. Something like this would never have been an inkling. This is on such a different level that I wouldn't have even thought about it, to be honest. This is completely above and beyond what I ever thought would happen. The Michael Bublé gig is an amazing thing to be a part of. The number of people that go into making it happen—really it is a small army of people. Luckily for us, it's an army of friends, from the carpenters on up. Everyone is tight-knit, close, a good gang of people. Aside from the fact that I couldn't even imagine being part of this, or I couldn't even believe that it really existed, is just the family that I have sort of inherited; and it is a good family.

What have you learned about your character as a result of being in this business?

That I am really stubborn! I'm going to do what I need to do, to get what I want. Not that I'll get it, but I will try to put a square peg through a round hole like it's no one's business. The most important thing for me, even back in my college days, was that I knew what I needed to do in order to further my career, to have the time to actually practice. A lot of the time, I tried to avoid taking a day job by going on a cruise ship, sacrificing my life for six months, playing sub-par music, just so I could have a respite when I came back, and I could just practice. So I had the long-term goal always in sight. It was never just, "Do this so I can get here." It was more like, "Okay, I have to get there. So in order to do that, I have a lot of work to do."

A lot of professional musicians spend most of their day just being me, me, me, me. Being an artist, you can be a very selfish person. And I know I have that in me. I've missed birthdays, anniversaries. Being a musician, you wind up missing a lot of stuff, making a sacrifice for doing what you want to do. It can be very selfish. And sometimes you get stuck in that mode, and you have to make that decision to have it not always be about you and your music all the time. That's, unfortunately, one of the side effects of this business that you can get stuck in. You have to have someone in your life who is willing to let you be gone a lot. And that's very selfish. It's something I am aware of but still get stuck in. That's just the nature of it. I think the funny thing is that music, when you are actually performing, is a gift. At least I like to think so. But at the same time, you are taking away from other people in your life. You are giving to some people, but then you are taking away from others. It's an interesting irony. So the fight not to be selfish is one that I want to develop within myself because I can be very selfish. It's something I am trying to deal with, and something I think a lot of musicians deal with.

Was there anyone who said that you wouldn't be able to make it in the music business—what was your response to him or her?

I know many people who were told that, but I actually never had that said to me, even by my parents. It's really funny because I ran into my best friend's parents not too long ago, and my friend's father told me that back when we were in high school, he had said to my dad, "Wow, Josh is really good!"

And evidently my dad replied, "Well, I know Josh is good, but I don't know if it is anything he'll ever be able to make a living at."

That really struck me because my dad never said that to me. I'm kind of glad they never shared that with me. It might have broken the romance of what I was doing.

In fact, if anything, I always felt that my parents, if not total stage parents, were very, very involved. They pushed me to be my best, as a musician. to do as much as I possibly could, with competitions and practicing. They were more than supportive of my music. In fact, I don't really know how I could be in the position I am in, if it hadn't been for them. Unfortunately, I know some people who had families that were not only not supportive, but totally against their becoming professional musicians. And a couple of them never turned out to be musicians. They just never did. They were very talented people, but it just didn't happen. I feel very fortunate that I didn't have that. I'm sure there were a couple of people thinking it! But they never really said it to me.

I am one of these people who at times have blinders on. If there is something I am interested in, I am really interested in it. If I'm not interested in it, which unfortunately is a lot of stuff, then I am totally blind to it. So I never graduated college thinking, "Okay, school is done, so now get out there and work." I just assumed that since I did music in school, I would do it for a living. Obviously, things weren't always that simple. I mean, I had my ups and downs, just like everyone does. There were certainly times when I was wondering where my next paycheck was going to come from.

But I never had anyone say I couldn't do it. I just had some people telling me to hustle more. Hustle more, practice, do all you can to get work. That doesn't stop. This isn't a career where you can just rest on your laurels and something else is just going to get handed to you. You have to go on auditions; you have to put yourself out there. Hopefully, you get to that stage, where, like a Wynton Marsalis, you always have something lining up for you.

I want to play. That's probably my most important thing. So I'm always trying to get to where I am always performing. And that's kind of the goal, to be playing the music that I want to play on a consistent enough basis to make a living.

Were there times when you thought that you might not make it yourself?

Fortunately enough, when I was young, I never thought in terms of making it or not making it. I just assumed that since it was something I had always done, I'd just continue. Of course, this was a fantasy that only a young person would think. Like many people, you realize that making it in your respective career choice is something in constant movement; doubt always sneaks into your mind. You can be fully prepared professionally, but luck, of course, always plays a small factor. So I never feel like I've made it and can just feel secure. I think anyone in the arts eventually has the realization that making it is something in the moment, when things are going well for you. It's hard to have a long career, and I think that is the real challenge. I think it's easier to have one hit TV show, or one hit album, or maybe a few years as a popular artist. I think longevity is the true goal. If I have a couple of weeks off from playing, I can sort of lose my purpose in life, and that's something I have to deal with.

What, for you, was the most unexpected aspect about being a professional musician?

The amount of travel that you have to do is crazy. If you want to be a touring musician, you can't mind flying.

If you were able, at this point in your life, to leave a note for your younger self when you were just starting out, what would the note say?

It would say: "You will be a goof off in your last year of high school and will hardly practice at all. Don't be an idiot! It will take years of practice to learn what you missed in that crucial year!"

Do you have a favorite quote that inspires or motivates you?

Not really, any thing from *The Big Lebowski* will do.

What does music mean to you?

To me, music is a feeling that you can't get anywhere else. It doesn't have to be one feeling—it can be many feelings—but it's a way to get a feeling that you can't get any other way. Reading, seeing a movie, interacting with another person—they just don't give you the same feeling that music does. It's your own personal experience, and you will feel it uniquely and differently from any other person.

Billy Kilson

✦

Birthdate: August 2, 1962

Birthplace: Washington, D.C.

Main instrument: Drums

Other instruments: Trumpet, trombone

Website: www.billykilson.com

How long have you been a professional musician?

I would say since 1987. My first professional gig was in Europe with a guy named Walter Davis, Jr. I was twenty-four, twenty-five at the time.

Have you had to support yourself with other jobs, or has music been your only profession?

I had some little speed bumps in the road. I started playing the drums at sixteen, and I went to Berklee College of Music right out of high school at eighteen-and-a-week years old. So at around nineteen, I thought, this is definitely no doubt what I want to do.

Most of my peers, men and women, were very successful. They were successful at an early age, before they were even twenty, or at twenty. That was the internal drive for me—I was

BILLY'S MUSICAL NOTES

♪ While continuing to tour with Chris Botti, Billy also leads his own band, Billy Kilson's BK Groove.

♪ Billy and his band have done three projects together, including an HD DVD/CD called *Rhythm Dancer* (Tuniverse, 2011).

♪ He plays on Dave Holland's Grammy-winning release *What Goes Around* (ECM Records, 2002), and his Grammy Award-nominated album *Prime Directive* (ECM Records, 2000).

♪ While playing drums, the one item Billy has to have along is chewing gum.

surrounded by success there. It was not happening to me, but I was surrounded by it.

But I had six years there [at Berklee], so what the heck did I do? I wasn't one of the lucky ones. I guess my mother would say I was fortunate because I'm one of the few that graduated from Berklee.

After that, I worked for the phone company. I had to pay my rent. I started gigging a bit late, later than most of my peers. I am two years younger than Branford Marsalis, and I went to school with him and a whole slew of jazz musicians who are in "Who's Who" right now. They were performing while they were students at Berklee. They were traveling around the world, and there I was, going to harmony class.

A lot of them left to go to New York, but I stayed in Boston, where Berklee is located, until I was twenty-six, twenty-seven—it was maybe eight or nine years that I stayed in Boston. So it was a bit late, at twenty-five, having my first professional gig. I had aspirations way before that, absolutely, five or six years before that.

What drew you to playing the drums?

I wish I had had the opportunity to make that choice, but they chose me. They said, "Hey, guy, come over here and sit down. We think you'll like these."

What drew you to jazz music?

It might be a slight on most music, but there's a limit, I think, on playing more pop, or funk, or rap, or whatever. There's a limit for the artist; there's a ceiling. By playing jazz, I wanted to expand my artistic ability. So that's what jazz did for me. It grabbed me, in a way, when I would hear these jazz drummers.

I grew up in a pop-oriented world. You can pick ten drummers in pop, or rock, or funk, and they each will have a different style, but something that they do will be somewhat similar. Not with jazz. You can have ten drummers, and they all come from—I don't know where! Where they hear these sounds, and how they are able to make their instruments sound that way! I guess more than anything else with drums and jazz, you have to have a sound, to play that music and to be pretty good—or to master the instrument.

I think that's what my goal was, once I went to Berklee. After I was there a semester or so, I decided I wanted to perfect this thing [drums] while I was on that quest, to try to get a unique sound out of the instrument, something all my own, which is so hard to do. So, in a nutshell, that is the reason—I wanted to master the instrument, and jazz is the vehicle that has taken me on that path.

Who played the most significant role in your musical development? Why?

From the start, it was my mom. What success I have, I owe to her. She supported me from day one. She taught me to stay focused, to have faith in myself and my abilities, and that anything is attainable.

And then there's Alan Dawson. Bar none, he's the guy who instilled my inner inspiration. I love the phrase this guy used once: "If it sounds good, it's all my teacher." So I would have to say, if there are any mistakes, that's all me—but if it sounds good, I have to say it's all Alan.

I went to Berklee to study with him. I had gone to this music camp my senior year in high school, and I wasn't sure where I wanted to go to college; this drummer was telling me I should go to Boston. He said there is this great teacher at Berklee College of Music, and he taught Tony Williams. He told me I should go see Alan, that Alan could help me. The one and only reason I went to Berklee was to study with Alan. But, when I got to Berklee, he had stopped teaching there. His last semester was in the spring prior to my fall semester. I freaked out! I didn't know what I was going to do. He was teaching at his home, which was ten, maybe fifteen, miles from Berklee. But he had a waiting list.

I didn't get to study with him for two years. It wasn't until I was twenty, maybe, that I got to study with him. This is not because of the waiting list, though. I went with some friends of mine to go see him play, during my first semester. Once I saw him, I thought, "No way could I study with that guy!" I grew up playing pop and funk music, and Alan Dawson was playing primarily jazz. It's like hearing English, English, English your whole life, and then walking into a place where everyone is speaking Russian or Arabic, and there's this kind of calligraphy on the wall. You're like, "Whoa! Wait!" So I thought, "No way am I going to study with him. I have to practice some more before I even ask this guy."

So, fast-forwarding a couple of years, I played at the Jazz Society Picnic. I was really into Philly Joe Jones at the time, so I had memorized everything that Philly Joe Jones played. Alan Dawson was playing at this picnic. I was playing with this band, and he was going to play later. He was off to the back and talking to someone while I was playing. I could see him slowly approaching the stage. So as I finished the solo, I walked off the stage, and he grabbed my left hand and asked me, "How are you able to play that without any formal training? It's obvious you haven't had any formal training. How are you able to play that, though?"

I said, "Well, Mr. Dawson, I practice with tapes, and I try to learn it."

He replied, "Come see me, and I can help you get to your destination much faster and much easier." That was his way of saying, "We'll skip everyone down the waiting list, and you can move to the front of the pack and come to my lessons." I was so moved, but I was freaked! Talk about a kid on Christmas Day! All my dreams came true.

I worked with pianist Ahmad Jamal in 1989, and even when I worked with him, I would call Alan from the road and say, "I don't know how to do this. What's happening with this? What do I need to do, to practice this?"

Towards the end of my apprenticeship, he stopped teaching me physically; I would just sit there for an hour, and we would exchange philosophical ideas. My lessons had graduated to that. Then, I still say, he kicked me out. My last lesson was almost like *Kung Fu* where the blind guy tells David Carradine, "If you can snatch the pebble from my hand, it will be time for you to leave." Alan gave me what they call the "ritual," which is the ultimate goal to achieve. That was the physical "snatch the pebble from the hand" moment, even though I still had a couple of years to go.

But since I was playing with Ahmad Jamal, Alan said, "There's nothing else I could really teach you, more than what you could learn from Ahmad Jamal." I felt like I was just getting started. Are you kidding? I was there for seven-and-a-half years, and I was learning so much from him. Of course there was the physical teaching, but I also was learning so much from him philosophically that was fruitful to my being a drummer and a musician.

But Alan was right in a sense because Ahmad Jamal is the third person I would say influenced me. Before I studied with him, I was just a drummer. After touring with him for over a year, I became a musician. So it's that trinity which influenced me the most: my mom, Alan Dawson, and Ahmad Jamal.

Is the life that you are living bigger than the one you had envisioned for yourself?

Yes, absolutely. I would say bigger and more rewarding. What's great about it is meeting people from four or five years old to forty or fifty years old, both men and women, who say that I've inspired them to play drums. And that's the bigger part of this platform I'm on now.

I thought I would feed myself on this fantasy of wanting to play onstage. I'm a kid when I'm onstage. All I wanted was just to do that. But I had no idea of the bigger part of it. I had no idea that my performance would touch someone. That never came to my mind. Are you kidding me? So it's much bigger.

In 2009, I had returned from a trip to Japan with the legendary pianist Hank Jones. Every night, someone would come up to me and say, "You're one of my biggest influences," or, "I love you," or, "I have that CD of yours." Somebody came up to me with a whole ditto sheet of all these CDs that I've played on, and I had absolutely no idea! So absolutely, it's bigger—much, much bigger.

What have you learned about your character as a result of being in this business?

I'm me. When you see me after a performance or whatever, I'm still me. I don't think I've changed. I grew up wanting to play basketball. I was okay, but I'm not six foot five. I realized that, when I was fifteen, "Okay I'm not growing anymore!" But I've always been outgoing and optimistic, even as pessimistic as I could have been when I was twenty-two, twenty-three, twenty-four, and thinking that this career thing is not going to happen. I've been like this, open-minded. When I'm onstage, I could be nine years old, I could be thirty-nine. It doesn't matter; it's me. I don't think I've changed significantly, besides my gray hair. The kid inside of me, that's the kid who plays the drums, for sure. And I take care of that little kid. So I always channel that kid inside of me, to stay grounded.

If there's anything weird, or that I didn't expect, is this whole travel thing. It's very, very hard. But it's all worth it. Like Chris [Botti] says sometimes, "You travel, take two flights that day, or whatever; it is crazy. But when we get onstage, the reward is when people are enthused with our performance. That's rewarding; it makes it all worth it." We forget all about the other stuff. I'm one of the fortunate people in that I have been able to achieve what I've always wanted to do. And I am thankful for that daily.

Although I have always wanted to play basketball, my mother, if she were still alive, would say, "This boy always wanted to play drums." I tore up all her furniture. I didn't get a drum set until I was sixteen, but everything you could think of, I was beating and banging on. I'm doing something I always wanted to do all my life. And I am very, very, very, very fortunate. Very fortunate.

Was there anyone who said that you wouldn't be able to make it in the music business—what was your response to him or her?

My peers were successful. My college roommate was a piano player, and during our second semester in college, he gets this phone call. (He had his own phone; he was pretty comfortable.) I answered the phone, and it was Kool from Kool & The Gang. He asked to talk with my roommate, and I told him that he was in class. He told me to tell him that Kool such-and-such called. I didn't even remember his last name, so I just said, "Whatever, Kool, whatever."

My roommate saw the note I left him, and when I got back from class, he said, "Do you know who that was?"

So then, during our third semester, I go home for Thanksgiving break, and my roommate was in the Thanksgiving Day Parade, playing with Kool & The Gang!

They nicknamed the time I went to Berklee, from 1978 to 1986, the "Golden Years of Berklee." That's where I met Mark Whitfield. If you check out "Who's Who in Jazz," I would say a good percentage of the guys who went to Berklee during that period of time are in it right now.

Of course, it would be easy to say that I was paranoid and thought that everyone was making it but me, but it was true! Realistically, twenty to thirty percent of the students at Berklee make it like that and are very successful. But in any kind of academia, whether it is high school, or you have a kid in Little League, or a kid that's an actor, it's only that one child from the school who becomes successful. So twenty percent is pretty big.

I did go to school with kids who, after one semester, decided that they just couldn't take it and said, "Oh, heck, no!" I wanted to do that, too, but I had too much pride. I couldn't go back home. And have my friends tease me? No way!

Were there times when you thought that you might not make it yourself?

I doubted it every day. Why did I keep doing it, is the question. I would have to say my faith in my teacher, Alan Dawson, and the perseverance and the wind beneath my wings, my mother. She'd say, "You've got to keep doing; you've got to keep trying."

I just kept trying because I doubted it every day. Heck, yeah. When I was twenty, twenty-one, and someone said to me that I'd be doing interviews, talking about my career, I'd have said, "No way, that's not going to happen." But I still practiced and dreamed every day.

That was the only drive that would get me to practice every

day: the bigger picture and the possibility I would obtain this
goal. But, realistically, it looked bleak, there. Every year was
winter, boy. A big snowstorm, a blizzard.

When I got to Berklee as a drummer, I had so much catching up to do. The drummer from *The Tonight Show*, Marvin
Smith, was two years ahead of me. His father played drums, so
he had started playing at age three. For a lot of these musicians,
someone in their family was musically inclined. The only thing
my family did was just play records on Saturdays. No one knew
anything about music. So I didn't think I was too paranoid—
they were a pretty successful group. And still are.

Now, for me, I make a living doing what I love to do. So, is
that equal with my peers? Yes. I said earlier that I wanted to
master the instrument. Hopefully, someday my contemporaries
are Max Roach, Philly Joe Jones, Elvin Jones and Tony Williams. Now my level of competition has been raised a bit because I've taken myself out of that box of "I just want a gig." It
is still in me that I want to master this instrument. So the level
now has become Miles Davis and Dizzy Gillespie, the legends
of jazz. I want to—not compete with them—but to sit at a table
with those guys.

My goal has shifted. I wanted to be able to perform and
make a living, and I've been able to do that. Plus, once I got to
the point where I could make a living, I was in my early thirties,
and I could take care of myself. I don't have to have a part-time
job, as well. Now that I'm a little older, I don't think, "Okay
I'm on this guy's level." It's just a whole different mindset,
now.

The ultimate goal is the simple proverbial thing that you
hear everyone say: I want to play better today than I played yes-
terday. I'm hoping that I play drums in a way that not only inspires other people to like the instrument, or like the music
that I'm attempting to perform, or the portrait that I'm attempting to paint, but also, I hope, as they leave, the performance
increases their respect for the instrument that I sit behind. It

could equal the respect that people have for the piano; I hope that changes. That's my lifelong goal, right now.

When you think of the drums, you think, "Okay, cool, anyone can just sit down and bang on them." The first instrument anyone will walk up to is the drums. Or they might sit behind a guitar, or something. But they will have a different respect for that piano. Everyone gets quiet when the piano plays. I would just love the drums to be on that same level, as a beautiful-sounding musical instrument. That's the goal. Every time I sit down, I'm hoping that someone says, "When Billy plays, it's something a little different. I didn't know that sound could come out of the drums." I'm hoping that their image [of the drums] is just changed slightly. When I inspire people, that's rewarding. That's when you know you've touched somebody. I'm still a student, but I'm getting there.

What, for you, was the most unexpected aspect about being a professional musician?

Touching so many strangers who have become my friends, worldwide, and not just in New York. It's my drumming (I never use that word) that is the catalyst that pulls people in. That's the biggest surprise. I never thought about that. And of course when I'm performing, I'm playing for me. But I'm hoping that you feel what I feel.

If you were able, at this point in your life, to leave a note for your younger self when you were just starting out, what would the note say?

Persevere. I am thinking of this nine-, ten-year-old kid who can barely spell it, but he should keep that word in his pocket and ask his mother, "What the heck does this mean?" She'd tell him what it means, but also say, "It must mean something else, too. So whatever you do, do that. Whatever it is; do *that*."

Do you have a favorite quote that inspires or motivates you?

I have this interview with Richard Pryor, whom I love. In a nutshell, Richard Pryor says, "The thoughts are yours, and the thoughts of yours are you." He said he's really not good with words; they come unnaturally to him. He likes to try and paint a picture, and that describes him better. So any of those thoughts or portraits, that's you. That's who you are.

Alan Dawson would always tell me that whenever I solo, I should want to paint a picture, not just get up there and bang. He'd tell me to set up this whole portrait, set up a frame. Don't just try to draw the audience in, have it also make sense. So when I heard this interview with Richard Pryor, that part stuck with me—he paints a picture. By the way, Richard Pryor played drums, too.

What does music mean to you?

Music is life to me. Bird [Charlie "Bird" Parker] said, "What you live comes through your horn." To me, what I live comes through that performance that day. However I function that day, whatever happened to me that day, or what has happened to me in life up until that point, is going to influence everything I have to say when I sit down behind the drums.

The thing that I love about music is that it transcends any race, any culture, any politics, and any religion. If it's performed purely, if it's from your heart, it is going to connect to someone who doesn't even like that kind of music. I can't count how many times people have said to me, "I hate the drums, and I never like to come to hear the drums, but my friend said I had to come see you. I told him, 'You know I hate the drums. I'm just going to go to sleep.' But you, you've changed that." That's my point. It transcends any barriers.

Music is life. For me, how I get through life is the strength of water. What I mean is that water is so strong, yet soft. You can't hold it in your hands, but it is strong enough to penetrate a rock. That's music for me; that's my artistry. That's my being, and I try to be like water—tangible. You can drink it, but it has that substance and strength of being able to penetrate anything. Anything.

Randy Napoleon

✦

Birthdate: May 30, 1977

Birthplace: Brooklyn

Main instrument: Guitar

Website: www.randynapoleon.com

How long have you been a professional musician?

I played my first gig as a leader when I was fifteen, and we all made ten dollars, I think. So that was the illustrious beginning of my career. I've been legitimately supporting myself by playing music since I was eighteen. I was lucky enough to get a scholarship to college, and I was able to pay for my incidentals and stuff by playing gigs.

I always had it in my heart that I wanted to move to New York. So many musicians that I looked up to and had listened to on records were in New York. I always knew that was the center of the music. I wanted to jump in the big pool to see if I could swim.

Something I have perspective on now is that there are excellent musicians scattered throughout the world. When I was growing up in Michigan, I had access to some really top-notch musicians, but the competitive aspect that New York has isn't there. In New York, you have twenty people that are at the top, on every instrument. Whatever kind of direction you want to go, there's going to be people to support it and to challenge you.

Have you had to support yourself with other jobs, or has music been your only profession?

It has all been music-related. There were a few years when I was teaching quite a bit. I love to teach and still have a few students. I've been fortunate that something gig-wise has always come up.

What drew you to the guitar?

I started off playing violin when I was in fifth grade in my school's instrumental music program, so I had some idea of how stringed instruments worked. But I wasn't seriously engaged or really passionate about that.

I had a friend who had a guitar, and he let me try it. I really remember holding the guitar and playing it the first time. I was immediately excited about it. He had two guitars, and I asked him if I could borrow his other guitar. I stayed up all night just trying to figure out a song. I did know that as you went up the fret board, the pitch was going to get higher. I had some idea of how stringed instruments worked, from the violin. I just started messing with the guitar. It was truly love at first sight!

What drew you to jazz music?

One of the things that made me want to be a jazz musician was when I heard the Ray Brown Trio while I was in high school. His trio had Benny Green on piano and Jeff Hamilton on drums, and they ended up being two of my early employers. I feel like I was preparing, specifically, for that sort of thing. Many of the gigs that I've gotten don't feel accidental for me;

RANDY'S MUSICAL NOTES

♪ Randy arranged most of Freddy Cole's Grammy-nominated record, *Freddy Cole Sings Mr. B.*, (High-Note, 2010).

♪ His hobbies include reading (either serious international politics or fantasy/science fiction), bike riding, and exploring new cities while on tour.

♪ He is enjoying life as a newlywed, with his wife, Alison.

they feel like where I was supposed to be, not that I feel like I could keep up with those guys in any way. I look up to them and am hoping that someday I can play a fraction as great as they play. I do feel that we had common direction. Maybe they picked up on the fact that I really loved their music, and I wanted to play in that direction.

There's some luck, too, but this whole process has a feeling of fate, almost from the first time I played the instrument. It feels like something that I am supposed to be doing.

Who played the most significant role in your musical development? Why?

There are my guitar heroes who I've been studying on records, but who I never got to meet because they were gone before I got into the music. My top two guitarists would be Wes Montgomery and Joe Pass. I'm never going to get tired of them!

Those kinds of influences are really important, but so are the people that you actually work with and develop with. I've got my teacher, and bandleaders that I've worked with. Rodney Whitaker and Paul Keller are both world-class bassists who live in Michigan, and they are as good as anyone in New York, hands-down. I love them. They are still my heroes, period.

I'm also influenced by my peers. I think we teach each other, people like Josh Brown, Ben Jansson and Jared Gold. These are guys that I've played with for years. We challenge each other; we argue about things; we share ideas. What do you think about this? Well, what do you think? It's more of a dialogue than it is with your teachers.

With your teachers, you are given someone's perspective, and you shut up and listen. You do it their way, and then you see how much of that works for you and what you would maybe do differently with your own group. But when you are with your peers, anything goes. It's like, "Let's try this." It may be horrible, but we try it together, and we learn and teach each other.

And then, of course, there is Freddy [Cole]. Being with Freddy is totally a dream gig. Freddy's book has got to be over a thousand songs. He'll just sit down at the piano and drop his hands, and we're into the set. You never know what's coming. He gives me a lot of room to play solos, and a lot of room to accompany, whatever I want to play that will fit. He doesn't want me to play the same stuff every night. He wants me to be creative with it.

Then there's Benny [Green], Jeff Hamilton, and John Clayton. They are the ones I've really absorbed what little I know about jazz from, and who have helped develop my tastes. Benny really spent a lot of time talking to me about music. That was really special.

Benny, more than anyone else, really made me aware of how far it was possible to go. He was very candid with me, in encouraging ways, about my potential, and he believed what I was working at was important. He was also painfully honest with me about what my current limitations were, and what I was going to have to do to get past them. Some of the things he would say to me were very hard to hear, but they were necessary, and the lessons were coming from someone who could demonstrate a better way. He really picked apart my playing. This was when I first moved to New York, and I was coming from Michigan, where I had always been praised, where it had been just victory after victory. It was a very humbling experience for me, but in a good way. It made it clear to me how large jazz is, and how much there is to explore.

Benny also set a real example of what it means to be passionate about music. We were in a van on tour somewhere, and some Wes Montgomery music came on. Wes is my favorite guitar player, so I said, "I love Wes Montgomery."

Benny looked at me and said something to me that I'll never forget, which was: "I need to hear the evidence in your playing that you love him." I thought that was really great because you hear people use the word "love" so casually about an artist, but what does it really mean to love them? It means that when you pick up your instrument, that love should shine through. Someone shouldn't have to wonder, "Where is he coming from?"

The way you do that is by digging deep into the music that you love and feel passionate about. Then it's naturally going to be processed out in a personal way. If you really invest yourself in somebody's music, you're not going to end up a clone. I can think of a couple of counter-examples to that, but to me they are unusual. I think if you are really passionate about something, you absorb it. It's like learning a language. You learn how to speak from your parents. You imitate word-by-word the way your parents talk. That's how you learn to enunciate; that's how you learn to construct a sentence. And that's how you learn to play jazz—through imitation of the people you love.

Everyone has influences. Even the greatest masters had influences. You can hear that Ray Brown came from Jimmy Blanton; you can hear it. You can hear that Wes Montgomery came from Charlie Christian. It's not a mystery. The beauty and the genius came from a personality and the fact that they kept adding on to it, putting their own spirit on top of it.

I can think of four of my favorite guitar players today who really love Wes Montgomery, right off the top of my head: Mark Whitfield, Russell Malone, Peter Bernstein, and George Benson. These guys clearly studied the hell out of Wes's music. And it is four different ways that it was processed through them, and it came out differently in all four cases. That's what it's about. That was something that really struck me.

I got into Benny's band when I first moved to New York. I was bouncing from sublet to sublet. Some of the landlords in New York won't let you sign a lease if you don't have a guarantor in the Tri-State Area [New York, New Jersey, Connecticut]. So, Benny let me stay with him for a couple of nights. I was sleeping under the piano so his cat wouldn't jump on me! Benny would get up, and he would practice for six, seven hours straight. I mean straight, not a rest. That would be just warming up his hands.

Benny was really intense. He put his money where his mouth was. He wasn't just someone who was resting on his laurels. He really, really puts his heart into the piano, and then it comes out when he plays. You can hear his influences because he's dug down deep enough to bring them out. So that's something I think about every day when I'm practicing. I think, "Okay, you say that you love this song or this guitar player. But how are you going to demonstrate that you love it? Are you going to prove that not through your words, but through your actions on the guitar?"

Is the life that you are living bigger than the one you had envisioned for yourself?

Everything measurable that I've thought I wanted to do, I've done. I've recorded CDs as a leader, I've toured as a leader, and I've toured with my heroes. I've played really large venues, really high-profile stuff. Everything that I could have described in words is done.

Now my definition of personal success mostly has to do with the music. I want to play the guitar better; I want to play it more consistently. I want to know that every time I pick up the guitar, it's going to be the best that I can give it. These are the bigger goals I dream of, now. It's just me versus my limitations, now.

On the business side, I want to get to the point where I am really well established, where I feel like I am the master of my own destiny. I want to be able to choose what I want to do and when I want to do it. I've been under the umbrellas of some major artists, and that's how I've been able to work. It's a lot different when people are coming to see you. That would be the next step. To be a part of all-star projects or my own group, where you feel like you have an identity of your own, in the business, something that you can support with your hands and your heart, something that's really personal and valuable on its own.

What have you learned about your character as a result of being in this business?

I've learned that my character can change if I will it to, hard enough. I've had battles with self-discipline, focus, keeping a positive attitude through hard times, self-acceptance of my limitations, acceptance of others' limitations, intellectual strength, physical strength, focusing while tired, etc. These are all works in progress, but my path in music has required growth in all of these areas and so many more.

I heard Herbie Hancock say one time that to be a better musician, you have to be a better person, and I certainly agree with him.

Was there anyone who said that you wouldn't be able to make it in the music business—what was your response to him or her?

Oh, yeah, everybody! Actually, I shouldn't say that *everybody* said I couldn't make it. My parents were very supportive. I had friends who were trying to do the same thing, and we all prodded and encouraged and supported each other. I had a very good environment growing up, and some older musicians were really great role models and very inspiring for me.

But when I started, I was really rough. It's been a slow burn for me, and I think I improve a little every year. I wasn't a child prodigy, or anything. Even though I was playing gigs when I was young, it was through a combination of a limited amount of talent and technique and a lot of "go-get-it" kind of energy. I was too ignorant to know what I didn't know.

Something that I love to think about now was when I told my high school counselor that I wanted to apply to music schools. He told me, "Your chances of becoming a professional musician are less than your chances of winning the lottery." So I took that as a healthy challenge.

I think now that this was actually good advice for a young aspiring musician to hear because if you are easily discouraged, you shouldn't do it. If that kind of obstacle, someone saying that to me, made me say to myself, "Okay maybe I shouldn't do it," then I shouldn't have. If that is enough to plant crippling doubt into your head, then there's just no way you are going to survive in New York with all this talent pouring out of the walls. How are you not going to lose your mind, if you can be discouraged by some high school counselor?

You've got to have a mix of confidence and insanity to want to do this. You can't let anyone tell you not to. I think that's the first thing someone should say to a person who is trying to be a professional musician: "Are you sure you want to do this? Because it is going to be hard." And if they say, "Well, I don't know. I don't know if I want to, if it is going to be hard," then they should forget it! Do something else. There are no guarantees, and it's not easy. It's wonderful, and it's satisfying, but only if you are really crazy in love with doing it. Not just that you *like* it, but that you can't keep your hands off the instrument, and you're going to go crazy if you are doing anything else.

There are times, when things are slow and you're not working, that you have to ask yourself: How much do I want this? How much do I believe I can do this? How much do I care? Could I do something else?

Because it's really easy to be positive when you are working. When it's tough, it's really tough. But there's no question for me. I can't do anything else. I don't mean I'm not capable; I just think about music all the time. I can't carry on a normal conversation because I'm always thinking about music. I'm really, really excited by it. It's the same excitement that I've had since day one. I'm still really excited by the guitar. I'm not a risk taker, but I just felt like I had no choice. I had to do it. If I had been on the fence, maybe that morning with my counselor would have steered me away. And it would have been a good thing because if you're on the fence, you're not going to succeed.

Were there times when you thought that you might not make it yourself?

I still doubt it sometimes. It's very discouraging, and there is always fear of what comes next. Even if you are on a good gig, you never really know what's going to happen next until you are deeply established, a household name, which I'm not. Part of that fear is healthy. It makes you practice and continue developing more things, to become more flexible. The more you can do, the better your odds are of survival.

Things are always changing, and I've been fortunate the last ten years to have had some really amazing opportunities. There are different things that made them all amazing. Getting to go on the road with Benny Green, that was incredible. It was like getting a really concentrated music lesson every single night. He is a flat-out genius, and he can articulate what he believes makes good music. Plus, he can really critique. That was just unbelievable for me.

It was the same kind of thing working with the Clayton-Hamilton Jazz Orchestra; it was an incredible learning experience.

The Bublé thing was more a band of my peers, and there were things that were incredible about that, too. Playing a really big concert every night helped me to get over some feelings of stage fright that I still had at that relatively late point in my career. If you are doing it every night, you can't get all tense. At some point it starts feeling like, "Okay, this is just another day at the office." Not that you don't get a little bit excited, and I think that's important so that you can bring some excitement to the job. But too many nerves can be debilitating. I used to feel sick to my stomach, and it would be hard for me to sleep before a big show.

That helped me because it was practicing a certain kind of thing—practicing getting comfortable with all the energy coming back from a large crowd. Also, having managers and business people running around helped me to get used to that kind of thing. Especially when we were doing all kinds of TV shows—it was really a lot of pressure. I think it was good, after a certain point, because I kind of got used to it.

What, for you, was the most unexpected aspect about being a professional musician?

I didn't realize that the challenges never end. Some of the guys, whom I look at as having made it, are still hungrier than you might think. For me, mostly, this has been just as I imagined it, the trials and all. I still love it, no question.

If you were able, at this point in your life, to leave a note for your younger self when you were just starting out, what would the note say?

Don't worry, you will find your way. As clichéd as it is, it's so important to follow your heart in music. That means you need to play the music that you love. You should listen to everyone around you because everyone is going to have some advice. Someone is going to say, "Well, this is what you really need to check out." And someone else is going to say, "No, that's crap." But at the end of the day, you have to know how you feel about music because there's no such thing as the greatest guitar player in the world. Or the greatest piano player. You can talk about maybe the fastest, or the person who has the biggest sound, or things like that. But that's not necessarily what you want to listen to. So the thing that is going to really define you as an artist is your particular taste. That means going after the stuff that you love. And if you love it, you're going to want to work at it hard because you care about it. If you don't really love it, that's an important thing to listen to, also.

Do you have a favorite quote that inspires or motivates you?

There is an Art Blakey quote: "Music washes away the dust of everyday life."

What does music mean to you?

Music is an expression of your whole life.

Peter Cincotti

Birthdate: July 11, 1983

Birthplace: New York City

Main instruments: Piano, vocals

Website: www.petercincotti.com

How long have you been a professional musician?

I started playing clubs in New York City when I was twelve or thirteen. I just started playing wherever there was a piano, whether it was a piano bar, a jazz club, a restaurant, or wherever. So I guess that would be my professional mark, around twelve or thirteen. My first paid gig was at a place called the Red Blazer, and I played with guys who were around four times my age. I remember learning a lot during that time. I might have earned a couple of dollars and a free Coke.

Have you had to support yourself with other jobs, or has music been your only profession?

I've been lucky enough to say that music has been my only profession.

What drew you to the piano?

I started playing when I was three years old and my grandmother bought me this toy piano. She taught me how to play "Happy Birthday" on it. Literally, I can't remember a time when I wasn't playing. It just kind of went from there.

Then we got a real piano in the house, and I played by ear for the first couple of years; then I started taking lessons.

No one else in my family played music as a profession, but my mother exposed my sister and me to all kinds of music and art throughout our childhood. Her father also had a great voice and was a singer. He was always singing around the house when he came over. It was a musical family. There was always music playing in the car, and in the house. We were influenced by a lot of music, especially growing up in New York. We saw all kinds of stuff, from Broadway shows, to rock concerts at Madison Square Garden, to jazz clubs, to theater, to whatever was here. We had a nice variety of music growing up. So New York City definitely played a role.

What drew you to jazz music?

I didn't really start getting into jazz until I was twelve or thirteen. I had played all kinds of music growing up. I had gone through phases of listening only to blues and early rock and roll, or piano rock and roll like Jerry Lee Lewis, Chubby Checker, Fats Domino, and even Elvis, though he wasn't playing piano. For some reason, early on, that fifties rock got me. That music is founded on the fundamentals of blues music, which I began playing soon after my "fifties rock" phase. Then from blues, I got into jazz.

I heard Oscar Peterson for the first time when I was in my early teens. That opened up a whole new door for me to all different kinds of piano players. Big influences for me were

PETER'S MUSICAL NOTES

♪ Peter is the youngest artist ever to reach number one on the Billboard Jazz Charts.

♪ At age seven, he played piano onstage with Harry Connick, Jr.

♪ Peter is a prize winner of the John Lennon Songwriting Contest.

♪ His acting credits include the movies *Spiderman 2* and *Beyond the Sea*.

Oscar Peterson and Erroll Garner, and early piano players like Fats Waller and Art Tatum, up until people like Keith Jarrett and Herbie Hancock. But the Oscar Peterson door was a big one for me.

I also played pop music along the way. In fact, the first song I ever wrote when I was nine was a pop song—a very pop song, almost like a Celine Dion-type pop song, believe it or not. I don't know where it came from, but pop music, for lack of a better term, was always something I played and explored from the very beginning. It was like a separate part of me that was always there, disconnected from my developments in blues and jazz. But, eventually, it all blended together.

Who played the most significant role in your musical development? Why?

I had a lot of influences and role models that were integral parts of my development, and the piano seemed to be at the core of all of them. Whether it was jazz piano players like the ones I just mentioned, or singer-songwriters like Stevie Wonder, Billy Joel, Elton John, and Randy Newman, or singer/piano players like Nat King Cole and Shirley Horn, they all played big roles in my development.

Ray Charles was a huge influence. He was someone that I idolized for a long time, especially with his effortless ability to somehow "swim" through genres. No matter what style he was playing, he was always Ray Charles, and to me musical identity is the most important thing. So he was a big one for me.

I was fortunate enough to meet Ray Charles once when I opened a show for him in Canada. It was a huge honor for me; it was right before he passed away. I did the first half, and then I got to watch his show right from the side of the stage, which was fascinating.

Watching him perform up close like that, I learned so

much. He had this huge big band, and he had no monitor system. I was wondering how he could hear himself sing in this large auditorium with this huge band. When I met him, I asked, "How do you hear yourself sing without any monitor?"

He said, "I like to hear what the people hear."

So, for the rest of my tour, I didn't use any monitors. But then, I realized I wasn't Ray Charles and put them back on stage!

Is the life that you are living bigger than the one you had envisioned for yourself?

I think it depends on how I look at it, and that changes. At times, it feels that way—when you're at the height of an album launch, when you're on tour, and when you're getting a "buzz"—because of things outside of the music that happen, like promotion and press. You're doing what you love in front of thousands of people. Yeah, then it feels bigger than what you'd hoped, or it feels like everything you would ever dream of.

But when you're playing in the middle of nowhere for half a house, and the band isn't together because you haven't had a show in a few months—that doesn't feel like a dream come true! There are ups and downs. But even when you wish there were more people in the crowd, that's okay, too. The bottom line is, I love to play music and perform. The audience is important, but it comes second.

What have you learned about your character as a result of being in this business?

I've learned that my character is what I want it to be. To a certain degree, you can only find that out when you are tested—

when you have to make decisions between music and money, or press and practice, or other decisions that involve a certain kind of sacrifice. Sometimes you need to choose between two opposing things, and as a result, you find out what's important to you by the decisions you are forced to make. And the harder the decision, the more you learn about yourself and your character.

Was there anyone who said that you wouldn't be able to make it in the music business—what was your response to him or her?

There were a couple of high school teachers, and even a few before that in grade school. I didn't really have good experiences in my school music classes. That's why I mostly studied privately. Hell, I even got kicked out of the jazz band in junior high school! The teachers, for some reason, always gave me a hard time.

Even when I was past that, and I started playing clubs in the city, I had a good amount of rejection early on. But you just have to keep plowing through it, I guess. The same people come around when you start to have success. So if you get there, you can have the last laugh—but by then, you don't even care, 'cause you're doing what you love, and those kinds of people suddenly don't matter anymore.

I remember keeping a list when I was in my early teens of all the people who wouldn't let me play in their clubs or in their restaurants. Some of them were just plain nasty about it. I actually kept the names of them all! A lot of them came back around when I did start to succeed a little bit, and I had my first record out. It's amazing how it works.

On the other hand, there are a lot of great people who give you the chance and are not afraid to share the stage with young people. I'm fortunate enough to have had a lot of those experiences, especially here in New York. I remember James

Williams, who has since passed away, as a great piano player, teacher, and generous man who would always share the stage.

I am also forever grateful to Harry Connick, Jr., who would always call me up on stage, from when I was around the age of seven until around fourteen. Whenever he was performing and he knew I was in the audience, he would call me up. Invaluable experiences like that are far more important than the rejections. Those are the experiences that fuel you to go forward and keep that fire alive inside you. Encouragement is really important.

Were there times when you thought that you might not make it yourself?

I had moments when I was down and would lose some confidence, but for the most part, I always knew I could do it. I still go through that because, for what I want to do in my career, a harder road is often required. Unfortunately, artistic development is something you have to fight for, and integrity is something you have to protect, especially nowadays. Formulas have always existed, and it is human nature to follow trends, but I believe it's harder to design something based on longevity today than it ever was.

My first record was a jazz record that went to the top of the charts and had a lot of success. The people around me at the time wanted me to make the same record again, for obvious reasons. Everybody was making money, and why fix what's not broken? But I wasn't interested in making the same record again. I wanted to move forward, for better or for worse.

It happened again when I went from my second record to my third record, which was my first album of all original material, and stylistically very different from either of my two previous records. I guess you could call it a pop record, but I hate that term. I went through a lot of people saying, "No, you're a jazz artist. You can't do this, and you can't do that."

David Foster, who produced my pop record, was a key element in my being able to make that jump—at least politically speaking. In the end it's all about the quality of music you make and the public reaction, but in order to get there, you need to put all the political pieces in the right place. Once David believed in me, then all these other people believed in me, and that was that. All of a sudden, I had support. So it trickles down.

The reason I play is really for me. On the one hand, it is selfish, but I think it needs to be. You need to love what you do before anyone else can love it. I think it's all about what success means to you, and everyone has different definitions. I never wanted to make musical decisions based on anything other than the music and what I felt. But the truth is, you end up making things a hell of a lot harder for yourself!

What, for you, was the most unexpected aspect about being a professional musician?

I remember when I first started, the thought of performing live, though it was something I wanted to do, was foreign. What happened over the course of a few years is that the stage became a second home, which in a way was a surprise. Now it's amazing to me how blurred it is. Now, when I perform on stage, there's a sense of being at home. It's very comfortable. The audience, and your initial idea of all those people out there, just changes.

The plane becomes your bedroom because you're taking so many flights when you're on tour. Your view of the world changes, too, because you get to see so many places. Yet you don't really get to see them. You're there, and you've gone all around the world, and you get home, and everyone says, "Wow, you were here, and you were there!" But you really weren't because you see the dressing room, and you see the backstage, and you see the hotel, and then you're off to the next city.

If you were able, at this point in your life, to leave a note for your younger self when you were just starting out, what would the note say?

Choose your battles.

Do you have a favorite quote that inspires or motivates you?

"Keep your friends close and your enemies closer," is pretty damn good.

What does music mean to you?

It's who I am. It's hard to differentiate at times. It's what I do, and I can't imagine my life without it.

Boney James

✦

Birthdate: September 1, 1961

Birthplace: Lowell, Massachusetts

Main instrument: Saxophone

Other instruments: Clarinet, keyboards

Website: www.boneyjames.com

How long have you been a professional musician?

My first real, serious job as a professional musician was when I was twenty-three. I had decided to become a professional musician when I was nineteen, during the summer between my freshman and sophomore years in college. I had studied history in college; I was thinking that maybe I was going to go into law school, or something like that. But going into my sophomore year, I realized I was not interested in anything other than music. I really loved music, and I thought I should give it a shot. But since I had already started towards this degree, I figured I should finish it because it's just part of my nature to finish things. So I was sort of getting this history degree

BONEY'S MUSICAL NOTES

♪ Boney is a three-time Grammy Award nominee for Best Pop Instrumental Album in 2001 and in 2004, and Best Traditional R&B Performance, in 2009. In 1998, his album, *Sweet Thing* (Warner/ WEA, 1997), received the Soul Train Award for Best Jazz Album .

♪ To date, nine of his albums have reached number one on the Billboard Contemporary Jazz Chart, and two have reached the top ten on the R&B Albums Chart, a rare accomplishment for an instrumental artist.

♪ Producer Quincy Jones is a major inspiration for Boney.

♪ He is married to actress-filmmaker Lily Mariye, who played Nurse Lily Jarvik on the TV series *ER* for fifteen seasons.

but playing in bands at night and dragging myself into class in the morning.

I loved music. I had always played in bands in high school, but it was more of a hobby. I didn't think it was possible to make a living as a musician. I was in a band when I was sixteen, and we had gotten a little record deal with an independent label, but it all fell apart at the last minute. I was really disillusioned by the business side of it. I thought it was so terrible, and I didn't want to put myself through that again—that disappointment and frustration that I felt.

Then, when I was nineteen and had just finished a year at college, I was going to school in Berkeley, California, and then came back to L.A. and started playing in another band over summer vacation. They had started playing around town in real club gigs, and I got up on the stage in a club. There was this epiphany that I had: This is really what I love doing! The college thing, studying history, really wasn't getting me excited. So I thought maybe this is what I should at least try to do.

That was when I decided that music was what I was really going to do. But I finished college, and then I had a number of years of struggling, trying to break into the business, before I was able to really start supporting myself as a musician. So, I was around twenty-three or twenty-four.

Have you had to support yourself with other jobs, or has music been your only profession?

After I graduated from college, I was delivering pizzas for a living. Even though music was exciting, and I was really happy to be pursuing this dream that I had, there were lots of frustrations. I really didn't enjoy being poor and working in the restaurant and all that stuff.

What drew you to playing the saxophone?

I was sort of browbeaten into being a sax player. I had been playing the clarinet for two years before that. I started the clarinet at age eight and only really picked up a clarinet because the music store didn't have any trumpets when I went. The trumpet was what I wanted, since all of my friends were playing it, but all they had were clarinets; so I had to take one. I had to take something; I was very impulsive.

I played clarinet for two years, and there were so many clarinet players in the band that the teacher picked me to switch to saxophone. I guess he thought I was the best clarinet player, so it would be easiest for me. I really didn't want to switch. He convinced me when he explained that the stage band in junior high school wouldn't have clarinet players in it; they would only have sax players in it. The stage band had just come to visit us in elementary school, and it was loud, and they had drums and electric guitars, plus they had snazzy satin jackets. So that's how he convinced me to switch to saxophone. I traded for a better outfit, essentially. But once I picked it up, I loved it. I really did.

What drew you to jazz music?

Sonically, I was never drawn to what most people consider to be straight-ahead jazz or be-bop; I love big band and swing. But Charlie Parker and stuff that a lot of people consider to be jazz, a lot of stuff that young traditional "jazzers" are doing now, is not something that I personally love. I always loved more song-oriented, more melody-oriented, groove-oriented, R&B kind of music. Music that really got me going was what we used to call fusion, when I was a kid, like Chick Corea or Pat Metheny. All the R&B hybrid things that were happening in the mid-seventies occurred when I was really getting into music.

Artists like Grover Washington, Jr. and George Benson were my roots, and straight-up R&B like Earth, Wind & Fire, Stevie Wonder, and Aretha Franklin—music like that.

My music is a real cross-section of different styles, the music that I ended up making as an artist. It has elements of jazz in it. The saxophone is certainly associated with jazz. There's improvisation, which I suppose is jazz. Jazz is such a nebulous term; what does it really mean? I never think of myself as a jazz musician, quite honestly. I'm more just a musician. That's part of living in this part of musical history. Things have melded quite a bit. Hopefully, there's not such a separation between genres. The business side wants to keep things separated, but a lot of the musicians I know just don't think in those terms.

Who played the most significant role in your musical development? Why?

A really pivotal year for me was 1975 to 1976. My family had just moved to California, and I was in high school. I was not happy about having to move away from all of my friends. That was also when I started turning towards music. When I first heard Earth, Wind & Fire, their *Gratitude* [Sony, 1975] record was really influential. Grover Washington, Jr.'s *Mister Magic* [Motown, 1974] record had just come out, and it was this incredible, vibrant R&B live sound. I listened to a lot of Grover, which is this beautiful-toned tenor saxophone and very improvisational, but it also has a melodic style, with this funky groove underneath it. So, I think that's probably the most influential year for me, musically, in terms of the music that I'm playing now. It probably still plays a huge part in the music that I make.

*Is the life that you are living bigger than the one you had envi-
sioned for yourself?*

Oh, yeah. I didn't even want to be a recording artist when I
first started. I thought I'd just be happy in the background as a
sideman and doing sessions and stuff like that. That was really
what I aspired to. I was much shyer back then, or I thought I
was. I didn't really know myself as well. I had this whole performer side that certainly was not apparent when I was
younger—to me, anyway. So I really just wanted to make a living
as a musician and kind of be off in the background.

But it evolved. I had seven years of touring as a sideman
and trying to break into the whole session world. I started to get
really frustrated with that. At first, I thought it was great that I
had started to make a living as a musician. But then I started to
feel frustrated with the musical side of it. For the most part, as a
touring musician, you are really just recreating things that other
people have put on records. That's really frustrating, and it got
sort of boring.

In terms of session work, I just wasn't getting the calls.
There is a real clique among the studio guys here in L.A., and I
was having a hard time breaking into it. That was one of the
main motives for making a record in the first place: If I make a
record as a sax player, I'll get noticed more, and I'll start doing
more sessions. People like Gerald Albright or Brandon Fields,
at the time, were the big session guys in town, and they had records out. So I thought, "Maybe I need to make a record." I
was getting known as a keyboard player/sax player guy, and I
really just wanted to play my sax more.

That was coupled with the fact that I was writing songs that
I really wanted people to hear. So, it was a twofold business
thing: to try to have this record, and to make it a calling card. I
was really surprised, when I started making my first record,
how much I loved having so much creative control over it and
the music in it. Also, just the act of making a record, expressing

myself via my music, as opposed to playing other people's music. So, it was like another light bulb went off over my head. It really wasn't until I started making my first record that I thought, "Wow, this is what I wanted to be—a recording artist." But at that time, did I envision being so successful? Absolutely not—I thought my mom would be the only one to buy it! I'm serious. I thought it was never going to work. There was a lot of competition at that time, too. The early nineties were a real booming time for sax records to be coming out.

For me, when I'm doing the work, I never think about other stuff, like how's it going to do, or is anybody going to notice it? I just try and make it sound good. I try and keep that in my head now, too, not to think so much about the outcome of it and just focus on the work, because that really is the fun part.

Besides, people don't want to hear records made from your scheming about how you are going to have a successful record. People want to hear records made out of love and commitment.

What have you learned about your character as a result of being in this business?

I learned that I'm really tenacious, and that I really do love performing. I really do, and I have this other side of my personality that comes out when I get on stage. Also, just that I am a really hard worker. I didn't realize that I was able to focus so much and to produce so much. Just to be at this point in my career, with such a big body of work; I've had twelve CDs and written all these songs over the years. I feel sort of prolific, which I never considered myself to be. I always had thought I was really slow. I had all these negative thoughts. It's been very affirming, actually, having this career.

On the negative side, I'm very impatient. That's one thing that this career has taught me about myself. But on a good day,

I'm able to separate myself from any sort of outcome and just focus on the work. Those are the really good days.

Was there anyone who said that you wouldn't be able to make it in the music business—what was your response to him or her?

I think that was mainly just me, if I have to honest about it. No one was really trying to steer me away from it.

Were there times when you thought that you might not make it yourself?

I probably just wasn't sure that it was viable. I thought I would just give it a shot. But once I made the decision at nineteen, twenty, I didn't really have doubts about it, at that point. I just thought I would sort of see how it goes.

I had lots of friends who were also trying to be musicians, and they were just dropping by the side of the road, going into other careers because they couldn't take it anymore. I just kept going. So I guess it's just a certain tenacity that I have. I don't remember exactly what my thought process was; it was just that whenever I was playing music, I knew that I was happy. So I thought, if I can be happy when I'm playing music, then maybe all this other stuff is worth it. That did turn out to be the case.

What, for you, was the most unexpected aspect about being a professional musician?

I'm always surprised that I'm doing it, that people have responded to my music in the way they ended up doing. That was surprising. I hadn't expected that at all.

Every day you can discover something musically, too. I still practice every day. Music itself is always surprising. I suppose it's surprising that I still have so much enthusiasm for doing it on a daily basis after all these years. Twenty-some-odd years as a professional musician, and I still feel as excited about it as when I started.

If you were able, at this point in your life, to leave a note for your younger self when you were just starting out, what would the note say?

You know, I've done a lot of things right, in a way, and why deny your younger self the ability to learn those lessons naturally? I don't know that I would want to say anything.

Do you have a favorite quote that inspires or motivates you?

I am not much of a quote kind of person. I don't think I have a favorite quote.

What does music mean to you?

Music is everything to me, it really is. It's just everything. It's my whole life.

Renee Olstead

✦

Birthdate: June 18, 1989

Birthplace: Houston

Main instrument: Vocals

Other instrument: Violin

Website: www.reneeolstead.com

How long have you been a professional musician?

I've been singing all my life, but I started singing with a big band when I was about twelve. We played gigs every weekend, and I was on a TV show at the time [*Still Standing*]—working pretty hard and having a good time.

Have you had to support yourself with other jobs, or has music been your only profession?

I've been lucky enough to have also found success on screen, first for four seasons on *Still Standing*, and now several seasons into *The Secret Life of the American Teenager*. I guess you could call jazz *my* secret life!

What drew you to singing jazz music?

I was watching the movie, *Pleasantville*, and the song "At Last" came on. It was the first time that the song connected with me. I've always been a musical person, but it was at that moment that I thought, "Wow, why can't I do that? I want to do that!"

Hearing it had a really profound impact on me. Sometimes you just don't know when things like that are going to happen.

Who played the most significant role in your musical development? Why?

I would say Billie Holiday is probably my biggest influence. I have her photograph on the wall with a big spotlight on it. She is always present in my house.

My second biggest influence, I would say, is Anita O'Day, whom I got to meet just before she passed away, which was really special for me. It was a screening for *Anita O'Day: The Life of a Jazz Singer,* which was a documentary on her life, a biopic. I was invited to the screening of it, and I got to meet her; though it was actually the second time we had met. It was meeting a legend, someone so much bigger than a person. I'll never forget it.

Is the life that you are living bigger than the one you had envisioned for yourself?

I feel like it is continually evolving. Sometimes, you don't know what is going to end up being the best choice, or what is going to end up being perfect for you. You just have to be open to change and open to ideas. I always hoped I would be suc-

RENEE'S MUSICAL NOTES

♪ At fifteen, Rence released her major label debut self-titled album, which included a duet with Peter Cincotti of "Breaking Up Is Hard to Do" (Reprise/WEA, 2004).

♪ Her follow-up album, *Skylark* (Reprise, 2009), features David Foster on strings, piano, horns, and keyboards.

♪ In 2006, Renee won a Young Artist Award for Best Performance in a TV Series for Comedy as Supporting Young Actress for her role in *Still Standing.*

♪ She currently stars as Madison in the TV series, *The Secret Life of the American Teenager*.

cessful; I mean everybody daydreams, right?
What have you learned about your character as a result of being in this business?

I think it has a lot to do with work ethics, for one. You should be very proactive. Obviously, being in the right place at the right time helps, but you have to follow through after that. You have to make a lot of sacrifices, as well.

Nothing is easy. Anything worth having is worth working for. I've had a lot of breaks in a very short amount of time, but at the same time, while I was on *Still Standing*, I was hauling my butt out to Malibu every night to record. There's no saying "no" to opportunities like that. They come once, and you have to know that.

Were there times when you thought that you might not make it in the music business?

Well, for myself, I've always been pretty realistic about the music industry and realized that it's a very fickle business. You can be really talented and not make it. I know plenty of amazing singers you'll never hear of, who sing in clubs, or I've seen perform, or who played with the band before I played with them. It's not fair, sometimes. You just have to factor that into the equation and know that sometimes it's not just being awesome; it's being awesome at the right place at the right time.

What, for you, was the most unexpected aspect about being a professional musician?

Waking up early enough to get everything you need accomplished in the daytime, when you have a workday that starts at ten at night.

If you were able, at this point in your life, to leave a note for your younger self when you were just starting out, what would the note say?

A note to myself would say, "Look for inspiration in everything."

Do you have a favorite quote that inspires or motivates you?

One of the most inspired feelings I ever had was when I listened to Billie Holiday's *Lady in Satin* [Sony, 1958] for the first time. That just blew my mind. I could feel everything that she was feeling right at that moment in the choices that she made with her voice. That was such a late album for her, in her career. It was the end, and you could hear it, and she knew it. It wasn't about her voice; it was about this feeling that she had.

What does music mean to you?

It means everything to me. It means happiness; it means sadness; it means expression. It means connecting with people. I connect with a lot of musicians, and it's really nice to be able to have something to connect you—no matter who they are, or where they're from, or what part of the country they grew up in. If you love music, and they love music, it connects you on this very basic and human level. It's amazing.

Bucky Pizzarelli

✦

Birthdate: January 9, 1926

Birthplace: Paterson, New Jersey

Main instrument: Guitar

Other instrument: Banjo

How long have you been a professional musician?

Since 1943. I was with the Vaughn Monroe band; it was a dance band. I was still in high school then. I was fortunate because I did a week with the band when I was off on Christmas vacation. Two weeks later, I graduated and went back with the band.

Have you had to support yourself with other jobs, or has music been your only profession?

It's the only thing I've ever done.

What drew you to playing the guitar?

BUCKY'S MUSICAL NOTES

♪ In 2011, Bucky was inducted into the New Jersey Hall of Fame.

♪ In 2005, he was one of the first musicians from New Jersey to have two of his guitars, along with a recorded history of his lifetime in music, included into the Smithsonian Institution in Washington, D.C.

♪ Bucky is a painter and has an extensive collection of more than one hundred pieces of his own artwork.

♪ His musical family includes sons John, a guitarist/vocalist, and Martin, a bassist, as well as daughters Mary, a guitarist, and Anne, a pianist.

In our family, we'd always play on Sundays. My uncles were good mandolin, banjo, and guitar players. I was probably around nine years old.

What drew you to jazz music?

My younger uncle, Bobby Domenick, played with a lot of dance bands, and I would forever see him coming on and off the road. It was always in the back of my mind to do that.

Who played the most significant role in your musical development? Why?

My two uncles started me off. They were both very good; they made a couple of great banjo records later in life, which were fabulous. First, they started me on banjo, but then they said I'd better get with the guitar because banjos are "out" now. And they were right!

Is the life that you are living bigger than the one you had envisioned for yourself?

No, my life is the same, the same Italian family. We do the same things we would do normally, even if I weren't doing music. My family would be the same.

What have you learned about your character as a result of being in this business?

That's all I thought about, was the music. I put that at the top of my list and said I wanted to do this. And then I went on to listen to all these great musicians that the band played with. Luckily, one guy was Joe Mooney, who was a blind jazz musician in Paterson, New Jersey. He played organ, piano and accordion. I had the chance to play with him a few times. He inspired me, and, musically, he was ahead of everyone else. To this day, I still have some of his harmonic sense in my playing and always give him credit for it.

Another thing is, you've got to look good when you play. You've got to dress up right. No matter how well you play, if you don't look right, you're not going to go over. And you're going to wonder why they don't hire you.

Was there anyone who said that you wouldn't be able to make it in the music business—what was your response to him or her?

No, nobody ever said that. I said to myself, "I'm going to make it." And that's what I did.

Were there times when you thought that you might not make it yourself?

No, I never did. I got into it, and then when you get with a band, you meet other musicians who are really good arrangers and conductors. You know what they expect, and you know what you fall short on. So, you just hone your skills and pick yourself up.

What, for you, was the most unexpected aspect about being a professional musician?

Meeting different people; I mean giants in the music

business, like Frank Sinatra. I've happened to play for three presidents: Bill Clinton, Richard Nixon, and Ronald Reagan. And I recently did a recording with Paul McCartney.

If you were able, at this point in your life, to leave a note for your younger self when you were just starting out, what would the note say?

I think everything I did worked out. I did it my way. I didn't go to music school. Kids go to college now to play. I don't think you have to do that. I play at music schools, and I see a lot of shortcomings. The kids ask these questions, and they don't know what to do with themselves. They all play the same four songs. It doesn't work that way. You've got to plug away; you've got to learn songs. You've got to have your own routine. And self-discipline.

Do you have a favorite quote that inspires or motivates you?

I always said the guitar is an accompaniment instrument. Your job is to make the other guys sound better. If you're playing with another guitar player, or you're playing for a singer, it's your job to make them sound good. I go with that attitude when I do a recording. It's not what you put in; it's what you leave out that makes it work.

What does music mean to you?

Everything, really. It never ends. You try to learn songs, but you can go your whole life and never learn them all. There's such beautiful music—classical, jazz. It's all the same.

Jason Moran

✦

Birthdate: January 21, 1975

Birthplace: Houston

Main instrument: Piano

Website: www.jasonmoran.com

How long have you been a professional musician?

Since 1996. It was a gig with the saxophonist Greg Osby. And I'm calling it professional because it was on an international scale.

Have you had to support yourself with other jobs, or has music been your only profession?

Music has been my only profession.

What drew you to playing the piano?

My parents. They thought playing an instrument was something, like chores, that you should do. At age six, who really thinks the piano is very interesting? It wasn't me, at least. I didn't think there was really any point.

I thought Thelonious Monk made it interesting sonically. At age twelve, I was not finding the simple Mozart or Bach pieces to be very interesting, especially in comparison to the hip-hop of the mid-eighties. So, at around thirteen, I heard Monk, and his music sounded extremely interesting to me.

What drew you to jazz music?

It was Monk, and it was also my parents.

Who played the most significant role in your musical development? Why?

It would be my parents, really. I would take these great jazz records from them; I would start scratching on them, too! My parents supported me in my endeavors. If I wanted to go to some jazz camp, they let me.

They let me set up my drum set in their living room, which left oil from the high hat on the rug. They let me set this up and leave it set up in the living room. I knew I had the freedom to make sound and not ever feel like I was cramping anyone's style by playing drums loudly, and badly, in the nice living room.

Is the life that you are living bigger than the one you had envisioned for yourself?

Oh yeah, much bigger. I always keep things in the ether. I would like to say things that I wanted, and then see if they would come true. So, a few months later, I got an audition letter from Betty Carter. They were having auditions for the Jazz Ahead program Betty created for young musicians. So I auditioned, they sent me an acceptance letter, and I said, "Oh,

JASON'S MUSICAL NOTES

♪ In 2010, Jason was named a MacArthur Fellow.

♪ His music is often influenced by edgy twentieth century painters, such as Glenn Ligon, Joan Jonas, Kara Walker, Adrian Piper, Jean-Michel Basquiat, Egon Schiele, and Robert Rauschenberg.

♪ Jason is passionate about modern furniture design, and when performing in the Tri-State area, he uses a chair custom built for him by Danish designer Susanne Forsgreen.

♪ He is married to mezzo-soprano Alicia Hall Moran, and they have twin sons.

wow! This is crazy!" I made a wishful statement, and it became true. It has actually happened multiple times in my career.

What have you learned about your character as a result of being in this business?

The good thing about my playing the music that I play is that the part of me that is unfocused can really express itself. Even when I'm playing a set of music, I'm not pooling from just one, or two, or three fragments of myself. Some of these subjects I might only know the surface of, but the synthesis of them all becomes something new.

Was there anyone who said that you wouldn't be able to make it in the music business—what was your response to him or her?

Oh yeah. I was in college at the Manhattan School of Music. There was a professor talking about chord changes and the scale you are supposed to use. I decided to try some of the ideas, which Greg [Osby] was discussing with me, in the class. When the teacher heard what I was trying, which was still using the kinds of information that he was giving us, he just stopped the class and said, "You can't play like that in this class. You can't do that in here."

I take things personally, so I was like, "First thing, Teacher, if you can explain to me what I'm doing, then I will totally do what you say to do. Here I am trying to do something that's new to me, and clearly new to you, and then all of sudden you call me out!" I can be pretty vulgar, and I just went off on him.

He was one example, and there were only a few others. People mostly just had good criticisms for me. That's always welcome. But he was the only one who ever said that I'd be lucky to have a twenty-five dollar gig.

Later in life, maybe six or seven years after I graduated and had four or five records out, this same teacher saw me and said that he was really proud of all of my accomplishments. I just smirked.

I try not to be that person that holds grudges because some people have bad days, and they say stupid stuff. I always still showed up for his class; I'm not that kind of person. I saved all my experimentation for other places, and that worked out better.

The whole thing I think about, being an instructor, is how do you balance criticism with also giving support? I never want to put out anyone's candle. I try and make it shine as bright as it can and, give it whatever I can that will help it shine brighter.

Were there times when you thought that you might not make it yourself?

I mean, yeah. When I was back at conservatory, I was going to leave school at the start of my junior year. I wasn't sure that music was for me. I didn't have any model for how a musician lived, what that lifestyle was, economically. My mother was an educator, and my father was an investment banker. I just didn't know how it was supposed to work and really just had to learn things. I started making a little bit of money, and I was still in New York and sharing my apartment with a roommate. When he moved out and I was still able to pay the rent, then I knew there was a possibility that I could make it.

What, for you, was the most unexpected aspect about being a professional musician?

That your dreams could come true. I never heard that when I was at the Manhattan School of Music. That any idea that you have, you actually have a possibility, if you meet the right people, and you play the right music, and you have a decent attitude. So that's been the big shock because everyone talks about artists, writers, choreographers, and how much they struggle. And I do know that it is a struggle; it is always a struggle. But what they don't tell you about is what the struggle is for: that when you do get to present something, whether it's your music, or you are playing a concert somewhere, the feeling of presenting your art is so gratifying. I didn't know that that was necessarily possible.

If you were able, at this point in your life, to leave a note for your younger self when you were just starting out, what would the note say?

It's gonna work. That's it. No matter what it was. Any of the things I was interested in as my younger self—I was into herpetology; I was into bass fishing. Those things will work. Any direction that I decided to go through as my younger self, it was going to work.

Do you have a favorite quote that inspires or motivates you?

"I'm serious about music, but I don't take it seriously." The quote is from Herbie Nichols.

What does music mean to you?

Music is a healing force in the universe. Albert Ayler has an album with a similar title.

THE INDEX